Second Thoughts
of an
Idle Fellow

*Other Jerome K. Jerome
titles from Alan Sutton Publishing*

Second Thoughts of an Idle Fellow
ISBN 0-86299-079-3

Three Men in a Boat
ISBN 0-86299-028-9

Three Men on the Bummel
ISBN 0-86299-029-7

Diary of a Pilgrimage
ISBN 0-86299-010-6

After Supper Ghost Stories
ISBN 0-86299-261-3

Tommy & Co.
ISBN 0-86299-174-9

My Life and Times
ISBN 0-86299-090-4

A Miscellany of Sense and Nonsense
ISBN 0-86299-080-7

Second Thoughts of an Idle Fellow

Jerome K. Jerome

Alan Sutton
1987

Alan Sutton Publishing Limited
Brunswick Road · Gloucester

First published 1898

Copyright © in this edition 1983
Alan Sutton Publishing Limited

Reprinted 1987

British Library Cataloguing in Publication Data

Jerome, Jerome K
  Second thoughts of an idle fellow.
  I. Title
  823′.8[E]   PR4825.J3

ISBN 0-86299-079-3

Typesetting and origination by
Alan Sutton Publishing Limited
Photoset 11/13 Imprint
Printed in Great Britain by
The Guernsey Press Company Limited,
Guernsey, Channel Islands.

CONTENTS

ON THE ART OF MAKING UP
ONE'S MIND

"Now, which would you advise, dear? You see, with the red I shan't be able to wear my magenta hat."

"Well then, why not have the grey?"

"Yes – yes, I think the grey will be *more useful*."

"It's a good material."

"Yes, and it's a *pretty* grey. You know what I mean, dear; not a *common* grey. Of course grey is always an *uninteresting* colour."

"It's quiet."

"And then again, what I feel about the red is that it is so warm-looking. Red makes you *feel* warm even when your're *not* warm. You know what I mean, dear."

"Well then, why not have the red? It suits you – red."

"No; do you really think so?"

"Well, when you've got a colour, I mean, of course."

"Yes, that *is* the drawback to red. No, I think, on the whole, the grey is *safer*."

"Then you will take the grey, madam?"

"Yes, I think I'd better; don't you, dear?"

"I like it myself very much."

"And it is good wearing stuff. I shall have it trimmed with – Oh! you haven't cut it off, have you?"

"I was just about to, madam."

"Well, don't for a moment. Just let me have another

7

look at the red. You see, dear, it has just occurred to me –
that chinchilla would look so well on the red."

"So it would, dear."

"And, you see, I've *got* the chinchilla."

"Then have the red. Why not?"

"Well, there is the hat I'm thinking of."

"You haven't anything else you could wear with that?"

"Nothing at all, and it would go so *beautifully* with the
grey. – Yes, I think I'll have the grey. It's always a safe
colour – grey."

"Fourteen yards I think you said, madam?"

"Yes, fourteen yards will be enough; because I shall
mix it with – One minute. You see, dear, if I take the
grey I shall have nothing to wear with my black jacket."

"Won't it go with grey?"

"Not well – not so well as with red."

"I should have the red then. You evidently fancy it
yourself."

"No, personally I prefer the grey. But then one must
think of *everything*, and – Good gracious! that's surely
not the right time?"

"No, madam, it's ten minutes slow. We always keep
our clocks a little slow."

"And we were to have been at Madame Jannaway's at a
quarter past twelve. How long shopping does take! Why,
whatever time did we start?"

"About eleven, wasn't it?"

"Half-past ten. I remember now; because, you know,
we said we'd start at half-past nine. We've been two
hours already!"

"And we don't seem to have done much, do we?"

"Done literally nothing, and I meant to have done *so*
much. I *must* go to Madame Jannaway's. Have you got
my purse, dear? Oh, it's all right, I've got it."

"Well, *now* you haven't decided whether you're going
to have the grey or the red."

"I'm sure I don't know what I *do* want now. I had
made up my mind a minute ago, and now it's all gone

again – oh yes, I remember, the red. Yes, I'll have the red. No, I don't mean the red, I mean the grey."

"You were talking about the red last time, if you remember, dear."

"Oh, so I was, you're quite right. That's the worst of shopping. Do you know I get quite confused sometimes."

"Then you will decide on the red, madam?"

"Yes – yes, I shan't do any better, shall I, dear? What do *you* think? You haven't got any other shades of red, have you? This is such an *ugly* red."

The shopman reminds her that she has seen all the other reds, and that this is the particular shade she selected and admired.

"Oh, very well," she replies, with the air of one from whom all earthly cares are falling, "I must take that then, I suppose. I can't be worried about it any longer. I've wasted half the morning already."

Outside she recollects three insuperable objections to the red, and four unanswerable arguments why she should have selected the grey. She wonders would they change it, if she went back and asked to see the shop-walker? Her friend, who wants her lunch, thinks not.

"That is what I hate about shopping," she says. "One never has time to really *think*."

She says she shan't go to that shop again.

We laugh at her, but are we so very much better? Come, my superior male friend, have *you* never stood, amid your wardrobe, undecided whether, in her eyes, you would appear more imposing, clad in the rough tweed suit that so admirably displays your broad shoulders; or in the orthodox black frock, that, after all, is perhaps more suitable to the figure of a man approaching – let us say, the nine-and-twenties? Or, better still, why not riding costume? Did we not hear her say how well Jones looked in his top-boots and breeches, and, "hang it all," we have a better leg than Jones. What a pity riding-breeches are made so baggy now-a-days. Why is it that male fashions tend more and more to hide the male leg? As women have become less and less ashamed of theirs, we have become more and more reticent of ours. Why are the silken hose, the tight-fitting pantaloons, the neat knee-breeches of our forefathers impossible to-day? Are we grown more modest – or has there come about a falling off, rendering concealment advisable?

I can never understand, myself, why women love us. It must be our honest worth, our sterling merit, that attracts them – certainly not our appearance, in a pair of tweed "dittos," black angora coat and vest, stand-up collar, and chimney-pot hat! No, it must be our sheer force of character that compels their admiration.

What a good time our ancestors must have had was borne in upon me when, on one occasion, I appeared in character at a fancy dress ball. What I represented I am unable to say, and I don't particularly care. I only know it was something military. I also remember that the costume was two sizes too small for me in the chest, and thereabouts; and three sizes too large for me in the hat. I padded the hat, and dined in the middle of the day off a chop and half a glass of soda-water. I have gained prizes as a boy for mathematics, also for scripture history – not often, but I have done it. A literary critic, now dead, once praised a book of mine. I know there have been occasions when my conduct has won the approbation of good men; but never – never in my whole life, have I felt more proud, more satisfied with myself than on that evening when, the last hook fastened, I gazed at my full-length Self in the cheval glass. I was a dream. I say it who should not; but I am not the only one who said it. I was a glittering dream. The groundwork was red, trimmed with gold braid wherever there was room for gold braid; and where there was no more possible room for gold braid there hung gold cords, and tassels, and straps. Gold buttons and buckles fastened me, gold embroidered belts and sashes caressed me, white horse-hair plumes waved o'er me. I am not sure that everything was in its proper place, but I managed to get everything on somehow, and I looked well. It suited me. My success was a revelation to me of female human nature. Girls who had hitherto been cold and distant gathered round me, timidly solicitous of notice. Girls on whom I smiled lost their heads and gave themselves airs. Girls who were not introduced to me sulked and were rude to girls that had been. For one poor child, with whom I sat out two dances (at least she sat, while I stood gracefully beside her – I had been advised, by the costumier, *not* to sit), I was sorry. He was a worthy young fellow, the son of a cotton broker, and he would have made her a good husband I feel sure. But he was foolish to come as a beer-bottle.

Perhaps, after all, it is as well those old fashions have gone out. A week in that suit might have impaired my natural modesty.

One wonders that fancy dress balls are not more popular in this grey age of ours. The childish instinct to "dress up," to "make believe," is with us all. We grow so tired of being always ourselves. A tea-table discussion, at which I once assisted, fell into this: – would any one of us, when it came to the point, change with anybody else, the poor man with the millionaire, the governess with the princess – change not only outward circumstances and surroundings, but health and temperament, heart, brain, and soul; so that not one mental or physical particle of one's original self one would retain, save only memory? The general opinion was that we would not, but one lady maintained the affirmative.

"Oh no, you wouldn't really, dear," argued a friend; "you *think* you would."

"Yes, I would," persisted the first lady; "I am tired of myself. I'd even be you, for a change."

In my youth, the question chiefly important to me was –What sort of man shall I decide to be? At nineteen one asks oneself this question; at thirty-nine we say, "I wish Fate hadn't made me this sort of man."

In those days I was a reader of much well-meant advice to young men, and I gathered that, whether I should become a Sir Lancelot, a Herr Teufelsdröckh, or an Iago was a matter for my own individual choice. Whether I should go through life gaily or gravely was a question the pros and cons of which I carefully considered. For patterns I turned to books. Byron was then still popular, and many of us made up our minds to be gloomy, saturnine young men, weary with the world, and prone to soliloquy. I determined to join them.

For a month I rarely smiled, or, when I did, it was with a weary, bitter smile, concealing a broken heart – at least that was the intention. Shallow-minded observers misunderstood.

"I know exactly how it feels," they would say, looking at me sympathetically, "I often have it myself. It's the sudden change in the weather, I think;" and they would press neat brandy upon me, and suggest ginger.

Again, it is distressing to the young man, busy burying his secret sorrow under a mound of silence, to be slapped on the back by common-place people and asked – "Well, how's the hump this morning?" and to hear his mood of dignified melancholy referred to, by those who should know better, as "the sulks."

There are practical difficulties also in the way of him who would play the Byronic young gentleman. He must be supernaturally wicked – or rather must *have been*; only, alas! in the unliterary grammar of life, where the future tense stands first, and the past is formed, not from the indefinite, but from the present indicative, "to have been" is "to be"; and to be wicked on a small income is impossible. The ruin of even the simplest of maidens costs money. In the Courts of Love one cannot sue *in formâ pauperis*; nor would it be the Byronic method.

"To drown remembrance in the cup" sounds well, but then the "cup," to be fitting, should be of some expensive brand. To drink deep of old Tokay or Asti is poetical; but when one's purse necessitates that the draught, if it is to be deep enough to drown anything, should be of thin beer at five-and-nine the four and a half gallon cask, or something similar in price, sin is robbed of its flavour.

Possibly also – let me think it – the conviction may have been within me that vice, even at its daintiest, is but an ugly, sordid thing, repulsive in the sunlight; that though – as rags and dirt to art – it may afford picturesque material to Literature, it is an evil-smelling garment to the wearer; one that a good man, by reason of poverty of will, may come down to, but one to be avoided with all one's effort, discarded with returning mental prosperity.

Be this as it may, I grew weary of training for a saturine young man; and, in the midst of my doubt, I chanced upon a book the hero of which was a debonnaire young buck, own cousin to Tom and Jerry. He attended fights, both of cocks and men, flirted with actresses, wrenched off door-knockers, extinguished street lamps, played many a merry jest upon many an unappreciative night watch-man. For all the which he was much beloved by the women of the book. Why should not I flirt with actresses, put out street lamps, play pranks on policemen, and be beloved? London life was changed since the days of my hero, but much remained, and the heart of woman is eternal. If no longer prize-fighting was to be had, at least there were boxing competitions, so called, in dingy back parlours out Whitechapel way. Though cock-fighting was a lost sport, were there not damp cellars near the river where for twopence a gentleman might back mongrel terriers to kill rats against time, and feel himself indeed a sportsman? True, the atmosphere of reckless gaiety, always surrounding my hero, I missed myself from these scenes, finding in its place an atmosphere more suggestive of gin, stale tobacco, and nervous apprehension of the police; but the essentials must have been the same, and the next morning I could exclaim in the very words of my prototype – "Odds crickets, but I feel as though the devil himself were in my head. Peste take me for a fool."

But in this direction likewise my fatal lack of means opposed me. (It affords much food to the philosophic mind, this influence of income upon character.) Even fifth-rate "boxing competitions," organized by "friendly leads," and ratting contests in Rotherhithe slums, become expensive, when you happen to be the only gentleman present possessed of a collar, and are expected to do the honours of your class in dog's-nose. True, climbing lamp-posts and putting out the gas is fairly cheap, providing always you are not caught in the act, but as a recreation it lacks variety. Nor is the modern London lamp-post adapted to sport. Anything more difficult to grip – anything with less "give" in it – I have rarely clasped. The disgraceful amount of dirt allowed to accumulate upon it is another drawback from the climber's point of view. By the time you have swarmed up your third post a positive distaste for "gaiety" steals over you. Your desire is towards arnica and a bath.

Nor in jokes at the expense of policemen is the fun entirely on your side. Maybe I did not proceed with judgment. It occurs to me now, looking back, that the neighbourhoods of Covent Garden and Great Marlborough Street were ill-chosen for sport of this nature. To bonnet a fat policeman is excellent fooling. While he is struggling with his helmet you can ask him comic questions, and by the time he has got his head free you are out of sight. But the game should be played in a district where there is not an average of three constables to every dozen square yards. When two other policemen, who have had their eye on you for the past ten minutes, are watching the proceedings from just round the next corner, you have little or no leisure for due enjoyment of the situation. By the time you have run the whole length of Great Titchfield Street and twice round Oxford Market, you are of opinion that a joke should never be prolonged beyond the point at which there is danger of its becoming wearisome; and that the time has now arrived for home and friends. The "Law," on the other hand, now raised by reinforcements to a strength of six or seven men, is just beginning to enjoy the chase. You picture to yourself, while doing Hanover Square, the scene in Court the next morning. You will be accused of being drunk and disorderly. It will be idle for you to explain to the magistrate (or to your relations afterwards) that you were only trying to live up to a man who did this sort of thing in a book and was admired for it. You will be fined the usual forty shillings; and on the next occasion of your calling at the Mayfields' the girls will be out, and Mrs. Mayfield, an excellent lady, who has always taken a motherly interest in you, will talk seriously to you and urge you to sign the pledge.

Thanks to your youth and constitution you shake off the pursuit at Notting Hill; and, to avoid any chance of unpleasant *contretemps* on the return journey, walk home to Bloomsbury by way of Camden Town and Islington.

I abandoned sportive tendencies as the result of a vow made by myself to Providence, during the early hours of a certain Sunday morning, while clinging to the waterspout of an unpretentious house situate in a side street off Soho. I put it to Providence as man to man. "Let me only get out of this," I think were the muttered words I used, "and no more 'sport' for me." Providence closed on the offer, and did let me get out of it. True, it was a complicated "get out," involving a broken skylight and three gas globes, two hours in a coal cellar, and a sovereign to a potman for the loan of an ulster; and when at last, secure in my chamber, I took stock of myself, – what was left of me, – I could not but reflect that Providence might have done the job neater. Yet I experienced no desire to escape the terms of the covenant; my inclining for the future was towards a life of simplicity.

Accordingly, I cast about for a new character, and found one to suit me. The German professor was becoming popular as a hero about this period. He wore his hair long and was otherwise untidy, but he had "a heart of steel," occasionally of gold. The majority of folks in the book, judging him from his exterior together with his conversation – in broken English, dealing chiefly with his dead mother and his little sister Lisa, – dubbed him uninteresting, but then they did not know about the heart. His chief possession was a lame dog which he had rescued from a brutal mob; and when he was not talking broken English he was nursing this dog.

But his speciality was stopping runaway horses, thereby saving the heroine's life. This, combined with the broken English and the dog, rendered him irresistible.

He seemed a peaceful, amiable sort of creature, and I decided to try him. I could not of course be a German professor, but I could, and did, wear my hair long in spite of much public advice to the contrary, voiced chiefly by small boys. I endeavoured to obtain possession of a lame dog, but failed. A one-eyed dealer in Seven Dials, to whom, as a last resource, I applied, offered to lame one for me for an extra five shillings, but this suggestion I declined. I came across an uncanny-looking mongrel late one night. He was not lame, but he seemed pretty sick; and, feeling I was not robbing anybody of anything very valuable, I lured him home and nursed him. I fancy I must have over-nursed him. He got so healthy in the end, there was no doing anything with him. He was an ill-conditioned cur, and he was too old to be taught. He became the curse of the neighbourhood. His idea of sport was killing chickens and sneaking rabbits from outside poulterers' shops. For recreation he killed cats and frightened small children by yelping round their legs. There were times when I could have lamed him myself, if only I could have got hold of him. I made nothing by running that dog – nothing whatever.

People, instead of admiring me for nursing him back to life, called me a fool, and said that if I didn't drown the brute they would. He spoilt my character utterly – I mean my character at this period. It is difficult to pose as a young man with a heart of gold, when discovered in the middle of the road throwing stones at your own dog. And stones were the only things that would reach and influence him.

I was also hampered by a scarcity in runaway horses. The horse of our suburb was not that type of horse. Once and only once did an opportunity offer itself for practice. It was a good opportunity, inasmuch as he was not running away very greatly. Indeed, I doubt if he knew himself that he was running away. It transpired afterwards that it was a habit of his, after waiting for his driver outside the Rose and Crown for what he considered to be a reasonable period, to trot home on his own account. He passed me going about seven miles an hour, with the reins dragging conveniently beside him. He was the very thing for a beginner, and I prepared myself. At the critical moment, however, a couple of officious policemen pushed me aside and did it themselves.

There was nothing for me to regret, as the matter turned out. I should only have rescued a bald-headed commercial traveller, very drunk, who swore horribly, and pelted the crowd with empty collar-boxes.

From the window of a very high flat I once watched three men, resolved to stop a runaway horse. Each man marched deliberately into the middle of the road and took up his stand. My window was too far away for me to see their faces, but their attitude suggested heroism unto death. The first man, as the horse came charging towards him, faced it with his arms spread out. He never flinched until the horse was within about twenty yards of him. Then, as the animal was evidently determined to continue its wild career, there was nothing left for him to do but to retire again to the kerb, where he stood looking

after it with evident sorrow, as though saying to himself –
"Oh, well, if you are going to be headstrong I have done
with you."

The second man, on the catastrophe being thus left
clear for him, without a moment's hesitation, walked up a
bye street and disappeared. The third man stood his
ground, and, as the horse passed him, yelled at it. I could
not hear what he said. I have not the slightest doubt it
was excellent advice, but the animal was apparently too
excited even to listen. The first and the third man met
afterwards, and discussed the matter sympathetically. I
judged they were regretting the pig-headedness of
runaway horses in general, and hoping that nobody had
been hurt.

I forget the other characters I assumed about this
period. One, I know, that got me into a good deal of
trouble was that of a downright, honest, hearty,
outspoken young man who always said what he meant.

I never knew but one man who made a real success of
speaking his mind. I have heard him slap the table with
his open hand and exclaim –

"You want me to flatter you – to stuff you up with a
pack of lies. That's not me, that's not Jim Compton. But
if you care for my honest opinion, all I can say is, that
child is the most marvellous performer on the piano I've
ever heard. I don't say she is a genius, but I have heard
Liszt and Metzler and all the crack players, and I prefer
her. That's my opinion. I speak my mind, and I can't
help it if you're offended."

"How refreshing," the parents would say, "to come
across a man who is not afraid to say what he really
thinks. Why are we not all outspoken?"

The last character I attempted I thought would be easy
to assume. It was that of a much admired and beloved
young man, whose great charm lay in the fact that he was
always just – himself. Other people posed and acted. He
never made any effort to be anything but his own
natural, simple self.

I thought I also would be my own natural, simple self. But then the question arose – What was my own natural, simple self?

That was the preliminary problem I had to solve; I have not solved it to this day. What am I? I am a great gentleman, walking through the world with dauntless heart and head erect, scornful of all meanness, impatient of all littleness. I am a mean-thinking, little-daring man – the type of man that I of the dauntless heart and the erect head despise greatly – crawling to a poor end by devious ways, cringing to the strong, timid of all pain. I – but, dear reader, I will not sadden your sensitive ears with details I could give you, showing how contemptible a creature this wretched I happens to be. Nor would you understand me. You would only be astonished, discovering that such disreputable specimens of humanity contrive to exist in this age. It is best, my dear sir, or madam, you should remain ignorant of these evil persons. Let me not trouble you with knowledge.

I am a philosopher, greeting alike the thunder and the sunshine with frolic welcome. Only now and then, when all things do not fall exactly as I wish them, when foolish, wicked people will persist in doing foolish, wicked acts, affecting my comfort and happiness, I rage and fret a goodish deal.

As Heine said of himself, I am knight, too, of the Holy Grail, valiant for the Truth, reverent of all women, honouring all men, eager to yield life to the service of my great Captain.

And next moment, I find myself in the enemy's lines, fighting under the black banner. (It must be confusing to these opposing Generals, all their soldiers being deserters from both armies.) What are women but men's playthings! Shall there be no more cakes and ale for me because thou art virtuous! What are men but hungry dogs, contending each against each for a limited supply of bones! Do others lest thou be done. What is the Truth but an unexploded lie!

I am a lover of all living things. You, my poor sister, struggling with your heavy burden on your lonely way, I would kiss the tears from your worn cheeks, lighten with my love the darkness around your feet. You, my patient brother, breathing hard as round and round you tramp the trodden path, like some poor half-blind gin-horse, stripes your only encouragement, scanty store of dry chaff in your manger! I would jog beside you, taking the strain a little from your aching shoulders; and we would walk nodding our heads side by side, and you, remembering, should tell me of the fields where long ago you played, of the gallant races that you ran and won. And you, little pinched brats, with wondering eyes, looking from dirt-encrusted faces, I would take you in my arms and tell you fairy stories. Into the sweet land of make-believe we would wander, leaving the sad old world behind us for a time, and you should be Princes and Princesses, and know Love.

But again, a selfish, greedy man comes often, and sits in my clothes. A man who frets away his life, planning how to get more money – more food, more clothes, more pleasures for himself; a man so busy thinking of the many things he needs he has no time to dwell upon the needs of others. He deems himself the centre of the universe. You would imagine, hearing him grumbling, that the world had been created and got ready against the time when he should come to take his pleasure in it. He would push and trample, heedless, reaching towards these many desires of his; and when, grabbing, he misses, he curses Heaven for its injustice, and men and women for getting in his path. He is not a nice man, in any way. I wish, as I say, he would not come so often and sit in my clothes. He persists that he is I, and that I am only a sentimental fool, spoiling his chances. Sometimes, for a while, I get rid of him, but he always comes back; and then he gets rid of me and I become him. It is very confusing. Sometimes I wonder if I really am myself.

ON THE DISADVANTAGE OF NOT GETTING WHAT ONE WANTS

Long, long ago, when you and I, dear Reader, were young, when the fairies dwelt in the hearts of the roses, when the moonbeams bent each night beneath the weight of angels' feet, there lived a good, wise man. Or rather, I should say, there had lived, for at the time of which I speak the poor old gentleman lay dying. Waiting each moment the dread summons, he fell a-musing on the life that stretched far back behind him. How full it seemed to him at that moment of follies and mistakes, bringing bitter tears not to himself alone but to others also. How much brighter a road might it have been, had he been wiser, had he known!

"Ah, me!" said the good old gentleman, "if only I could live my life again in the light of experience."

Now as he spoke these words he felt the drawing near to him of a Presence, and thinking it was the One whom he expected, raising himself a little from his bed, he feebly cried, "I am ready."

But a hand forced him gently back, a voice saying, "Not yet; I bring life, not death. Your wish shall be granted. You shall live your past life again, and the knowledge of the past shall be with you to guide you. See you use it. I will come again."

Then a sleep fell upon the good man, and when he awoke, he was again a little child, lying in his mother's arms; but, locked within his brain was the knowledge of the life that he had lived already.

So once more he lived and loved and laboured. So a second time he lay an old, worn man with life behind him. And the angel stood again beside his bed; and the voice said,

"Well, are you content now?"

"I am well content," said the old gentleman. "Let Death come."

"And have you understood?" asked the angel.

"I think so," was the answer; "that experience is but as of the memory of the pathways he has trod to a traveller journeying ever onward into an unknown land. I have been wise only to reap the reward of folly. Knowledge has oft-times kept me from my good. I have avoided my old mistakes only to fall into others that I knew not of. I have reached the old errors by new roads. Where I have escaped sorrow I have lost joy. Where I have grasped happiness I have plucked pain also. Now let me go with Death that I may learn."

Which was so like the angel of that period, the giving of a gift, bringing to a man only more trouble. Maybe I am over-rating my coolness of judgment under somewhat startling circumstances, but I am inclined to think that, had I lived in those days, and had a fairy or an angel come to me, wanting to give me something – my soul's desire, or the sum of my ambition, or any trifle of that kind – I should have been short with him.

"You pack up that precious bag of tricks of yours," I should have said to him (it would have been rude, but that is how I should have felt), "and get outside with it. I'm not taking anything in your line to-day. I don't require any supernatural aid to get me into trouble. All the worry I want I can get down here, so it's no good your calling. You take that little joke of yours, – I don't know what it is, but I know enough not to want to know, – and run it off on some other idiot. I'm not priggish. I have no objection to an innocent game of 'catch-questions' in the ordinary way, and when I get a turn myself. But if I've got to pay every time, and the stakes are to be my earthly happiness plus my future existence – why I don't play. There was the case of Midas; a nice, shabby trick you fellows played off upon him! making pretence you did not understand him, twisting round the poor old fellow's words, just for all the world as though you were a pack of Old Bailey lawyers, trying to trip up a witness; I'm ashamed of the lot of you, and I tell you so – coming down here, fooling poor unsuspecting mortals with your nonsense, as though we had not enough to harry us as it was. Then there was that other case of the poor old peasant couple to whom you promised three wishes, the whole thing ending in a black pudding. And they never got even that. You thought that funny, I suppose. That was your fairy humour! A pity, I say, you have not, all of you, something better to do with your time. As I said before, you take that celestial 'Joe Miller' of yours and work if off on somebody else. I have read my fairy lore, and I have read my mythology, and I don't want any of your blessings. And what's more, I'm not going to have them. When I want blessings I will put up with the usual sort we are accustomed to down here. You know the ones I mean, the disguised brand – the blessings that no human being would think were blessings, if he were not told; the blessings that don't look like blessings, that don't feel like blessings; that, as a matter of fact, are *not* blessings, practically speaking; the blessings that other people think are blessings for us and that we don't. They've got their drawbacks, but they are better than yours, at any rate, and they are sooner over. I don't want your blessings at any price. If you leave one here I shall simply throw it out after you."

I feel confident I should have answered in that strain, and I feel it would have done good. Somebody ought to have spoken plainly, because with fairies and angels of that sort fooling about, no one was ever safe for a moment. Children could hardly have been allowed outside the door. One never could have told what silly trick some would-be funny fairy might be waiting to play off on them. The poor child would not know, and would think it was getting something worth having. The wonder to me is that some of those angels didn't get tarred and feathered.

I am doubtful whether even Cinderella's luck was quite as satisfying as we are led to believe. After the carpetless kitchen and the black beetles, how beautiful the palace must have seemed – for the first year, perhaps for the first two. And the Prince! how loving, how gallant, how tender – for the first year, perhaps for the first two. And after? You see he was a Prince, brought up in a Court, the atmosphere of which is not conducive to the development of the domestic virtues; and she – was Cinderella. And then the marriage altogether was rather a hurried affair. Oh yes, she is a good, loving little woman; but perhaps our Royal Highness-ship did act too much on the impulse of the moment. It was her dear, dainty feet that danced their way into our heart. How they flashed and twinkled, cased in those fairy slippers. How like a lily among tulips she moved that night amid the over-gorgeous Court dames. She was so sweet, so fresh, so different to all the others whom we knew so well. How happy she looked as she put her trembling little hand in ours. What possibilities might lie behind those drooping lashes. And we were in amorous mood that night, the music in our feet, the flash and glitter in our eyes. And then, to pique us further, she disappeared as suddenly and strangely as she had come. Who was she? Whence came she? What was the mystery surrounding her? Was she only a delicious dream, a haunting phantasy that we should never look upon again, never clasp again within our longing arms? Was our heart to be for ever hungry, haunted by the memory of – No, by heavens, she is real, and a woman. Here is her dear slipper, made surely to be kissed. Of a size too that a man may well

wear within the breast of his doublet. Had any woman –
nay, fairy, angel, such dear feet! Search the whole
kingdom through, but find her, find her. The gods have
heard our prayers, and given us this clue. "Suppose she
be not all she seemed. Suppose she be not of birth fit to
mate with our noble house!" Out upon thee, for an
earth-bound, blind curmudgeon of a Lord High Chancellor. How could a woman, whom such slipper fitted, be
but of the noblest and the best, as far above us, mere
Princelet that we are, as the stars in heaven are brighter
than thy dull old eyes! Go, search the kingdom, we tell
thee, from east to west, from north to south, and see to it
that thou findest her, or it shall go hard with thee. By
Venus, be she a swineherd's daughter, she shall be our
Queen – an she deign to accept of us, and of our
kingdom.

Ah well, of course, it was not a wise piece of business,
that goes without saying; but we were young, and Princes
are only human. Poor child, she could not help her
education, or rather her lack of it. Dear little thing, the
wonder is that she has contrived to be no more ignorant
than she is, dragged up as she was, neglected and
overworked. Nor does life in a kitchen, amid the com-
panionship of peasants and menials, tend to foster the
intellect. Who can blame her for being shy and somewhat
dull of thought? not we, generous-minded, kind-hearted
Prince that we are. And she is very affectionate. The
family are trying, certainly; father-in-law not a bad sort,
though a little prosy when upon the subject of his
domestic troubles, and a little too fond of his glass;
mamma-in-law, and those two ugly, ill-mannered sisters,
decidedly a nuisance about the palace. Yet what can we
do? they are our relations now, and they do not forget to
let us know it. Well, well, we had to expect that, and
things might have been worse. Anyhow she is not jealous
– thank goodness.

So the day comes when poor little Cinderella sits alone
of a night in the beautiful palace. The courtiers have

gone home in their carriages. The Lord High Chancellor has bowed himself out backwards. The Gold-Stick-in-Waiting and the Grooms of the Chamber have gone to their beds. The Maids of Honour have said "Good-night," and drifted out of the door, laughing and whispering among themselves. The clock strikes twelve – one – two, and still no footstep creaks upon the stair. Once it followed swiftly upon the "good-night" of the maids, who did not laugh or whisper then.

At last the door opens, and the Prince enters, none too pleased at finding Cinderella still awake. "So sorry I'm late, my love – detained on affairs of state. Foreign policy very complicated, dear. Have only just this moment left the Council Chamber."

And little Cinderella, while the Prince sleeps, lies sobbing out her poor sad heart into the beautiful royal pillow, embroidered with the royal arms and edged with the royal monogram in lace. "Why did he ever marry me? I should have been happier in the old kitchen. The black beetles did frighten me a little, but there was always the dear old cat; and sometimes, when mother and the girls were out, papa would call softly down the kitchen stairs for me to come up, and we would have such a merry evening together, and sup off sausages: dear old dad, I hardly ever see him now. And then, when my work was done, how pleasant it was to sit in front of the fire, and dream of the wonderful things that would come to me some day. I was always going to be a Princess, even in my dreams, and live in a palace, but it was so different to this. Oh, how I hate it, this beastly palace where everybody sneers at me – I know they do, though they bow and scrape, and pretend to be so polite. And I'm not clever and smart as they are. I hate them. I hate these bold-faced women who are always here. That is the worst of a palace, everybody can come in. Oh, I hate everybody and everything. Oh, god-mamma, god-mamma, come and take me away. Take me back to my old kitchen. Give me back my old poor frock. Let me dance again with the fire-tongs for a partner, and be happy, dreaming."

Poor little Cinderella, perhaps it would have been better had god-mamma been less ambitious for you, dear; had you married some good, honest yeoman, who would never have known that you were not brilliant, who would have loved you because you were just amiable and pretty; had your kingdom been only a farmhouse, where your knowledge of domestic economy, gained so hardly, would have been useful; where you would have shone instead of being overshadowed; where Papa would have dropped in of an evening to smoke his pipe and escape from his domestic wrangles; where you would have been *real* Queen.

But then you know, dear, you would not have been content. Ah yes, with your present experience – now you know that Queens as well as little drudges have their troubles; but *without* that experience? You would have looked in the glass when you were alone; you would have looked at your shapely hands and feet, and the shadows would have crossed your pretty face. "Yes," you would have said to yourself – "John is a dear, kind fellow, and I love him very much, and all that, but –" and the old dreams, dreamt in the old low-ceilinged kitchen before the dying fire, would have come back to you, and you would have been discontented then as now, only in a different way. Oh yes, you would, Cinderella, though you gravely shake your gold-crowned head. And let me tell you why. It is because you are a woman, and the fate of all us, men and women alike, is to be for ever wanting what we have not, and to be finding, when we have it, that it is not what we wanted. That is the law of life, dear. Do you think as you lie upon the floor with your head upon your arms, that you are the only woman whose tears are soaking into the hearthrug at that moment? My dear Princess, if you could creep unseen about your City, peeping at will through the curtain-shielded windows, you would come to think that all the world was little else than a big nursery full of crying children with none to comfort them. The doll is broken: no longer it sweetly squeaks in answer to our pressure, "I love you, kiss me." The drum lies silent with the drumstick inside; no longer do we make a brave noise in the nursery. The box of tea-things we have clumsily put our foot upon; there will be no more merry parties around the three-legged stool. The tin trumpet will not play the note we want to sound; the wooden bricks keep falling down; the toy cannon has exploded and burnt our fingers. Never mind, little man, little woman, we will try and mend things to-morrow.

And after all, Cinderella dear, you do live in a fine palace, and you have jewels and grand dresses and – No, no, do not be indignant with *me*. Did not you dream of these things *as well as* of love? Come now, be honest. It was always a prince, was it not; or, at the least, an exceedingly well-to-do party, that handsome young gentleman who bowed to you so gallantly from the red embers? He was never a virtuous young commercial traveller, or cultured clerk, earning a salary of three pounds a week, was he, Cinderella? Yet there are many charming commercial travellers, many delightful clerks with limited incomes, quite sufficient, however, to a sensible man and woman desiring but each other's love. Why was it always a prince, Cinderella? Had the palace and the liveried servants, and the carriages and horses, and the jewels and the dresses, *nothing* to do with the dream?

No, Cinderella, you were human, that is all. The artist, shivering in his conventional attic, dreaming of Fame! – do you think he is not hoping she will come to his loving arms in the form Jove came to Danae? Do you think he is not reckoning also upon the good dinners and the big cigars, the fur coat and the diamond studs, that her visits will enable him to purchase?

There is a certain picture very popular just now. You may see it, Cinderella, in many of the shop-windows of the town. It is called "The Dream of Love," and it represents a beautiful young girl, sleeping in a very beautiful but somewhat disarranged bed. Indeed, one hopes, for the sleeper's sake, that the night is warm, and that the room is fairly free from draughts. A ladder of light streams down from the sky into the room, and upon this ladder crowd and jostle one another a small army of plump Cupids, each one laden with some pledge of love. Two of the Imps are emptying a sack of jewels upon the floor. Four others are bearing, well displayed, a magnificent dress (a "confection," I believe, is the proper term) cut somewhat low, but making up in train what is lacking elsewhere. Others bear bonnet boxes from which peep stylish toques and bewitching hoods. Some, representing evidently wholesale houses, stagger under silks and satins in the piece. Cupids are there from the shoemakers with the daintiest of *bottines*. Stockings, garters, and even less mentionable articles, are not forgotton. Caskets, mirrors, twelve-buttoned gloves, scent-bottles and handkerchiefs, hair-pins, and the gayest of parasols, has the God of Love piled into the arms of his messengers. Really a most practical, up-to-date God of Love, moving with the times! One feels that the modern Temple of Love must be a sort of Swan and Edgar's; the god himself a kind of celestial shop-walker; while his mother, Venus, no doubt superintends the costume department. Quite an Olympian Whiteley, this latter-day Eros; he has forgotten nothing, for, at the back of the picture, I notice one Cupid carrying a rather fat heart at the end of a string.

You, Cinderella, could give good counsel to that sleeping child. You would say to her – "Awake from such dreams. The contents of a pawnbroker's store-room will not bring you happiness. Dream of love if you will; that is a wise dream, even if it remain ever a dream. But these coloured beads, these Manchester goods! are you then – you, heiress of all the ages – still at heart only as some poor savage maiden but little removed above the monkeys that share the primeval forest with her? Will you sell your gold to the first trader that brings you *this* barter? These things, child, will only dazzle your eyes for a few days. Do you think the Burlingon Arcade is the gate of Heaven?"

Ah, yes, I too could talk like that – I, writer of books, to the young lad, sick of his office stool, dreaming of a literary career leading to fame and fortune. "And do you think, lad, that by that road you will reach Happiness sooner than by another? Do you think interviews with yourself in penny weeklies will bring you any satisfaction after the first half-dozen? Do you think the gushing female who has read all your books, and who wonders what it must feel like to be so clever, will be welcome to you the tenth time you meet her? Do you think press cuttings will always consist of wondering admiration of your genius, of paragraphs about your charming personal appearance under the heading, 'Our Celebrities'? Have you thought of the *un*complimentary criticisms, of the spiteful paragraphs, of the everlasting fear of slipping a few inches down the greasy pole called 'popular taste,' to which you are condemned to cling for life, as some lesser criminal to his weary tread-mill, struggling with no hope but not to fall! Make a home, lad, for the woman who loves you; gather one or two friends about you; work, think, and play, that will bring you happiness. Shun this roaring gingerbread fair that calls itself, forsooth, the 'World of art and letters.' Let its clowns and its contor-tionists fight among themselves for the plaudits and the halfpence of the mob. Let it be with its shouting and its surging, its blare and its cheap flare. Come away, the summer's night is just the other side of the hedge, with its silence and its stars."

You and I, Cinderella, are experienced people, and can therefore offer good advice, but do you think we should be listened to?

"Ah, no, my Prince is not as yours. Mine will love me always, and I am peculiarly fitted for the life of a palace. I have the instinct and the ability for it. I am sure I was made for a princess. Thank you, Cinderella, for your well-meant counsel, but there is much difference between you and me."

That is the answer you would receive, Cinderella; and my young friend would say to me, "Yes, I can understand *your* finding disappointment in the literary career; but then, you see, our cases are not quite similar. *I* am not likely to find much trouble in keeping *my* position. *I* shall not fear reading what the critics say of *me*. No doubt there are disadvantages, when you are among the ruck, but there is always plenty of room at the top. So thank you, and good-bye."

Besides, Cinderella dear, we should not quite mean it – this excellent advice. We have grown accustomed to these gew-gaws, and we should miss them in spite of our knowledge of their trashiness: you, your palace and your little gold crown; I, my mountebank's cap, and the answering laugh that goes up from the crowd when I shake my bells. We want everything. All the happiness that earth and heaven are capable of bestowing. Creature comforts, and heart and soul comforts also; and, proud-spirited beings that we are, we will not be put off with a part. Give us only everything, and we will be content. And, after all, Cinderella, you have had your day. Some little dogs never get theirs. You must not be greedy. You have *known* happiness. The palace was Paradise for those few months, and the Prince's arms were about you, Cinderella, the Prince's kisses on your lips; the gods themselves cannot take *that* from you.

The cake cannot last for ever if we will eat of it so greedily. There must come the day when we have picked hungrily the last crumb – when we sit staring at the empty board, nothing left of the feast, Cinderella, but the pain that comes of feasting.

It is a naïve confession, poor Human Nature has made to itself, in choosing, as it has, this story of Cinderella for its leading moral:– Be good, little girl. Be meek under

your many trials. Be gentle and kind, in spite of your
hard lot, and one day – you shall marry a prince and ride
in your own carriage. Be brave and true, little boy. Work
hard and wait with patience, and in the end, with God's
blessing, you shall earn riches enough to come back to
London town and marry your master's daughter.

You and I, gentle Reader, could teach these young
folks a truer lesson, an we would. We know, alas! that the
road of all the virtues does not lead to wealth, rather the
contrary; else how explain our limited incomes? But
would it be well, think you, to tell them bluntly the truth
– that honesty is the most expensive luxury a man can
indulge in; that virtue, if persisted in, leads, generally
speaking, to a six-roomed house in an outlying suburb?
Maybe the world is wise: the fiction has its uses.

I am acquainted with a fairly intelligent young lady.
She can read and write, knows her tables up to six times,
and can argue. I regard her as representative of average
Humanity in its attitude towards Fate; and this is a
dialogue I lately overheard between her and an older lady
who is good enough to occasionally impart to her the
wisdom of the world –

"I've been good this morning, haven't I?"

"Yes – oh yes, fairly good, for you."

"You think Papa *will* take me to the circus to-night?"

"Yes, if you keep good. If you don't get naughty this
afternoon."

A pause.

"I was good on Monday, you may remember, nurse."

"Tolerably good."

"*Very* good, you said, nurse."

"Well, yes, you weren't bad."

"And I was to have gone to the pantomime, and I
didn't."

"Well, that was because your aunt came up suddenly,
and your Papa couldn't get another seat. Poor auntie
wouldn't have gone at all if she hadn't gone then."

"Oh, wouldn't she?"

"No."

Another pause.

"Do you think she'll come up suddenly to-day?"

"Oh no, I don't think so."

"No, I hope she doesn't. I want to go to the circus to-night. Because, you see, nurse, if I don't it will discourage me."

So, perhaps the world is wise in promising us the circus. We believe her at first. But after a while, I fear, we grow discouraged.

ON THE EXCEPTIONAL MERIT ATTACHING TO THE THINGS WE MEANT TO DO

I can remember – but then I can remember a long time ago. You, gentle Reader, just entering upon the prime of life, that age by thoughtless youth called middle, I cannot, of course, expect to follow me – when there was in great demand a certain periodical ycleped *The Amateur*. Its aim was noble. It sought to teach the beautiful lesson of independence, to inculcate the fine doctrine of self-help. One chapter explained to a man how he might make flower-pots out of Australian meat cans; another how he might turn butter-tubs into music-stools; a third how he might utilize old bonnet boxes for Venetian blinds: that was the principle of the whole scheme, you made everything from something not intended for it, and as ill-suited to the purpose as possible.

Two pages, I distinctly recollect, were devoted to the encouragement of the manufacture of umbrella stands out of old gas-piping. Anything less adapted to the receipt of hats and umbrellas than gas-piping I cannot myself conceive: had there been, I feel sure the author would have thought of it, and would have recommended it.

Picture-frames you fashioned out of ginger-beer corks. You saved your ginger-beer corks, you found a picture – and the thing was complete. How much ginger-beer it would be necessary to drink, preparatory to the making of each frame; and the effect of it upon the frame-maker's physical, mental, and moral well-being, did not concern *The Amateur*. I calculate that for a fair-sized picture sixteen dozen bottles might suffice. Whether, after sixteen dozen of ginger-beer, a man would take any interest in framing a picture – whether he would retain any pride in the picture itself, is doubtful. But this, of course, was not the point.

One young gentleman of my acquaintance – the son of the gardener of my sister, as friend Ollendorff would have described him – did succeed in getting through sufficient ginger-beer to frame his grandfather, but the result was not encouraging. Indeed, the gardener's wife herself was but ill satisfied.

"What's all them corks round father?" was her first question.

"Can't you see," was the somewhat indignant reply, "that's the frame."

"Oh! but why corks?"

"Well, the book said corks."

Still the old lady remained unimpressed.

"Somehow it don't look like father now," she sighed.

Her eldest born grew irritable: none of us appreciate criticism!

"What does it look like, then?" he growled.

"Well, I dunno. Seems to me to look like nothing but corks."

The old lady's view was correct. Certain schools of art possibly lend themselves to this method of framing. I myself have seen a funeral card improved by it; but, generally speaking, the consequence was a predominance of frame at the expense of the thing framed. The more honest and tasteful of the frame-makers would admit as much themselves.

"Yes, it is ugly when you look at it," said one to me, as we stood surveying it from the centre of the room. "But what one feels about it is that one has done it oneself."

Which reflection, I have noticed, reconciles us to many other things beside cork frames.

Another young gentleman friend of mine – for I am bound to admit it was youth that profited most by the advice and counsel of *The Amateur*: I suppose as one grows older one grows less daring, less industrious – made a rocking-chair, according to the instructions of this book, out of a couple of beer barrels. From every practical point of view it was a bad rocking-chair. It rocked too much, and it rocked in too many directions at one and the same time. I take it, a man sitting on a rocking-chair does not want to be continually rocking. There comes a time when he says to himself – "Now I have rocked sufficiently for the present; now I will sit still for a while, lest a worse thing befall me." But this was one of those headstrong rocking-chairs that are a danger to humanity, and a nuisance to themselves. Its notion was that it was made to rock, and that when it was *not* rocking, it was wasting its time. Once started nothing could stop it – nothing ever did stop it, until it found itself topsy turvy on its own occupant. That was the only thing that ever sobered it.

I had called, and had been shown into the empty drawing-room. The rocking-chair nodded invitingly at me. I never guessed it was an amateur rocking-chair. I was young in those days, with faith in human nature, and I imagined that, whatever else a man might attempt without knowledge or experience, no one would be fool enough to experiment upon a rocking-chair.

I threw myself into it lightly and carelessly. I immediately noticed the ceiling. I made an instinctive movement forward. The window and a momentary glimpse of the wooded hills beyond shot upwards and disappeared. The carpet flashed across my eyes, and I caught sight of my own boots vanishing beneath me at the rate of about two hundred miles an hour. I made a convulsive effort to recover them. I suppose I over-did it. I saw the whole of the room at once, the four walls, the ceiling, and the floor at the same moment. It was a sort of vision. I saw the cottage piano upside down, and I again saw my own boots flash past me, this time over my head, soles uppermost. Never before had I been in a position where my own boots had seemed so all-pervading. The next moment I lost my boots, and stopped the carpet with my head just as it was rushing past me. At the same instant something hit me violently in the small of the back. Reason, when recovered, suggested that my assailant must be the rocking-chair. Investigation proved the surmise correct. Fortunately I was still alone, and in consequence was able, a few minutes later, to meet my hostess with calm and dignity. I said nothing about the rocking-chair. As a matter of fact, I was hoping to have the pleasure, before I went, of seeing some other guest arrive and sample it: I had purposely replaced it in the most prominent and convenient position. But though I felt capable of schooling myself to silence, I found myself unable to agree with my hostess when she called for my admiration of the thing. My recent experiences had too deeply embittered me.

"Willie made it himself," explained the fond mother. "Don't you think it was very clever of him."

"Oh yes, it was clever," I replied, "I am willing to admit that."

"He made it out of some old beer barrels," she continued; she seemed proud of it.

My resentment, though I tried to keep it under control, was mounting higher.

"Oh! did he?" I said; I should have thought he might have found something better to do with them."

"What?" she asked.

"Oh! well, many things," I retorted. "He might have filled them again with beer."

My hostess looked at me astonished. I felt some reason for my tone was expected.

"You see," I explained, "it is not a well-made chair. These rockers are too short, and they are too curved, and one of them, if you notice, is higher than the other and of a smaller radius; the back is at too obtuse an angle. When it is occupied the centre of gravity becomes —"

My hostess interrupted me.

"You have been sitting on it," she said.

"Not for long," I assured her.

Her tone changed. She became apologetic.

"I am so sorry," she said. "It looks all right."

"It does," I agreed; "that is where the dear lad's cleverness displays itself. Its appearance disarms suspicion. With judgment that chair might be made to serve a really useful purpose. There are mutual acquaintances of ours – I mention no names, you will know them – pompous, self-satisfied, superior persons who would be improved by that chair. If I were Willie I should disguise the mechanism with some artistic drapery, bait the thing with a couple of exceptionally inviting cushions, and employ it to inculcate modesty and diffidence. I defy any human being to get out of that chair, feeling as important as when he got into it. What the dear boy has done has been to construct an automatic exponent of the transitory nature of human greatness. As a moral agency that chair should prove a blessing in disguise."

My hostess smiled feebly; more, I fear, from politeness than genuine enjoyment.

"I think you are too severe," she said. "When you remember that the boy has never tried his hand at anything of the kind before, that he has no knowledge and no experience, it really is not so bad."

Considering the matter from that point of view I was bound to concur. I did not like to suggest to her that before entering upon a difficult task it would be better for young men to *acquire* knowledge and experience: that is so unpopular a theory.

But the thing that *The Amateur* put in the front and foremost of its propaganda was the manufacture of household furniture out of egg-boxes. Why egg-boxes I have never been able to understand, but egg-boxes, according to the prescription of *The Amateur*, formed the foundation of household existence. With a sufficient supply of egg-boxes, and what *The Amateur* termed a "natural deftness," no young couple need hesitate to face the furnishing problem. Three egg-boxes made a writing-table; on another egg-box you sat to write; your books were ranged in egg-boxes around you – and there was your study, complete.

For the dining-room two egg-boxes made an overmantel; four egg-boxes and a piece of looking-glass a sideboard; while six egg-boxes, with some wadding and a yard or so of cretonne, constituted a so-called "cosy corner." About the "corner" there could be no possible doubt. You sat on a corner, you leant against a corner; whichever way you moved you struck a fresh corner. The "cosiness," however, I deny. Egg-boxes I admit can be made useful; I am even prepared to imagine them ornamental; but "cosy," no. I have sampled egg-boxes in many shapes. I speak of years ago, when the world and we were younger, when our fortune was the Future; secure in which, we hesitated not to set up house upon incomes folks with lesser expectations might have deemed insufficient. Under such circumstances, the sole alternative to the egg-box, or similar school of furniture, would have been the strictly classical, consisting of a doorway joined to architectural proportions.

I have from Saturday to Monday, as honoured guest, hung my clothes in egg-boxes. I have sat on an egg-box at an egg-box to take my dish of tea. I have made love on egg-boxes. – Aye, and to feel again the blood running through my veins as then it ran, I would be content to sit only on egg-boxes till the time should come when I could be buried in an egg-box, with an egg-box reared above me as tombstone. – I have spent many an evening on an egg-box; I have gone to bed in egg-boxes. They have their points – I am intending no pun – but to claim for them cosiness would be but to deceive.

How quaint they were, those home-made rooms! They rise out of the shadows and shape themselves again before my eyes. I see the knobbly sofa; the easy-chairs that might have been designed by the Grand Inquisitor himself; the dented settle that was a bed by night; the few blue plates, purchased in the slums off Wardour Street; the enamelled stool to which one always stuck; the mirror framed in silk; the two Japanese fans crossed beneath each cheap engraving; the piano cloth embroidered in peacock's feathers by Annie's sister; the tea-cloth worked by Cousin Jenny. We dreamt, sitting on those egg-boxes – for we were young ladies and gentlemen with artistic taste – of the days when we would eat in Chippendale dining-rooms; sip our coffee in Louis Quatorze drawing-rooms; and be happy. Well, we have got on, some of us, since then, as Mr. Bumpus used to say; and I notice, when on visits, that some of us have contrived so that we do sit on Chippendale chairs, at Sheraton dining-tables, and are warmed from Adam's fireplaces; but, ah me, where are the dreams, the hopes, the enthusiasms that clung like the scent of a March morning about those gim-crack second floors? In the dustbin, I fear, with the cretonne- covered egg-boxes and the penny fans. Fate is so terribly even-handed. As she gives she ever takes away. She flung us a few shillings and hope, where now she doles us out pounds and fears. Why did not we know how happy we were, sitting crowned with sweet conceit upon our egg-box thrones?

Yes, Dick, you have climbed well. You edit a great newspaper. You spread abroad the message – well, the message that Sir Joseph Goldbug, your proprietor, instructs you to spread abroad. You teach mankind the lessons that Sir Joseph Goldbug wishes them to learn. They say he is to have a peerage next year. I am sure he has earned it; and perhaps there may be a knighthood for you, Dick.

Tom, you are getting on now. You have abandoned those unsaleable allegories. What rich art patron cares to be told continually by his own walls that Midas had ass's ears; that Lazarus sits ever at the gate? You paint portraits now, and everybody tells me you are the coming man. That "Impression" of old Lady Jezebel was really wonderful. The woman looks quite handsome, and yet it *is* her ladyship. Your touch is truly marvellous.

But into your success, Tom – Dick, old friend, do not there creep moments when you would that we could fish up those old egg-boxes from the past, refurnish with them the dingy rooms in Camden Town, and find again there our youth, our loves, and our beliefs?

An incident brought back to my mind, the other day, the thought of all these things. I called for the first time upon a man, an actor, who had asked me to come and see him in the little home where he lives with his old father. To my astonishment – for the craze, I believe, has long since died out – I found the house half furnished out of packing cases, butter tubs, and egg-boxes. My friend earns his twenty pounds a week, but it was the old father's hobby, so he explained to me, the making of these monstrosities; and of them he was as proud as though they were specimen furniture out of the South Kensington Museum.

He took me into the dining-room to show me the latest outrage – a new book-case. A greater disfigurement to the room, which was otherwise prettily furnished, could hardly be imagined. There was no need for him to assure me, as he did, that it had been made out of nothing but egg-boxes. One could see at a glance that it was made out of egg-boxes, and badly constructed egg-boxes at that – egg-boxes that were a disgrace to the firm that had turned them out; egg-boxes not worthy the storage of "shop'uns" at eighteen the shilling.

We went up-stairs to my friend's bedroom. He opened the door as a man might open the door of a museum of gems.

"The old boy," he said, as he stood with his hand upon the door-knob, "made everything you see here, everything," and we entered. He drew my attention to the wardrobe. "Now I will hold it up," he said, "while you pull the door open; I think the floor must be a bit uneven, it wobbles if you are not careful." It wobbled notwithstanding, but by coaxing and humouring we succeeded without mishap. I was surprised to notice a very small supply of clothes within, although my friend is a dressy man.

"You see," he explained, "I dare not use it more than I can help. I am a clumsy chap, and as likely as not, if I happened to be in a hurry, I'd have the whole thing over:" which seemed probable.

I asked him how he contrived. "I dress in the bath-room as a rule," he replied; "I keep most of my things there. Of course the old boy doesn't know."

He showed me a chest of drawers. One drawer stood half open.

"I'm bound to leave that drawer open," he said; "I keep the things I use in that. They don't shut quite easily, these drawers; or rather, they shut all right, but then they won't open. It is the weather, I think. They will open and shut all right in the summer, I dare say." He is of a hopeful disposition.

But the pride of the room was the washstand.

"What do you think of this?" cried he enthusiastically, "real marble top —"

He did not expatiate further. In his excitement he had laid his hand upon the thing, with the natural result that it collapsed. More by accident then design I caught the jug in my arms. I also caught the water it contained. The basin rolled on its edge and little damage was done, except to me and the soap-box.

I could not pump up much admiration for this washstand; I was feeling too wet.

"What do you do when you want to wash?" I asked, as together we reset the trap.

There fell upon him the manner of a conspirator revealing secrets. He glanced guiltily round the room;

then, creeping on tip-toe, he opened a cupboard behind the bed. Within was a tin basin and a small can.

"Don't tell the old boy," he said. "I keep these things here, and wash on the floor."

That was the best thing I myself ever got out of egg-boxes – that picture of a deceitful son stealthily washing himself upon the floor behind the bed, trembling at every footstep lest it might be the "old boy" coming to the door.

One wonders whether the Ten Commandments are so all-sufficient as we good folk deem them – whether the eleventh is not worth the whole pack of them: "that ye love one another" with just a common-place, human, practical love. Could not the other ten be comfortably stowed away into a corner of that! One is inclined, in one's anarchic moments, to agree with Louis Stevenson, that to be amiable and cheerful is a good religion for a work-a-day world. We are so busy *not* killing, *not* stealing, *not* coveting out neighbour"s wife, we have not time to be even just to one another for the little while we are together here. Need we be so cocksure that our present list of virtues and vices is the only possibly correct and complete one? Is the kind, unselfish man necessarily a villain because he does not always succeed in suppressing his natural instincts? Is the narrow-hearted, sour-souled man, incapable of a generous thought or act, necessarily a saint because he has none? Have we not – we unco guid – arrived at a wrong method of estimating our frailer brothers and sisters? We judge them, as critics judge books, not by the good that is in them, but by their faults. Poor King David! What would the local Vigilance Society have had to say to him? Noah, according to our plan, would be denounced from every teetotal platform in the country, and Ham would head the Local Vestry poll as a reward for having exposed him. And St. Peter! weak, frail St. Peter, how lucky for him that his fellow-disciples and their Master were not as strict in their notions of virtue as are we to-day.

Have we not forgotten the meaning of the word "virtue"? Once it stood for the good that was in a man, irrespective of the evil that might lie there also, as tares among the wheat. We have abolished virtue, and for it substituted virtues. Not the hero – he was too full of faults – but the blameless valet; not the man who does any good, but the man who has not been found out in any evil, is our modern ideal. The most virtuous thing in nature, according to this new theory, should be the oyster. He is always at home, and always sober. He is not noisy. He gives no trouble to the police. I cannot think of a single one of the Ten Commandments that he ever breaks. He never enjoys himself, and he never, so long as he lives, gives a moment's pleasure to any other living thing.

I can imagine the oyster lecturing a lion on the subject of morality.

"You never hear me," the oyster might say, "howling round camps and villages, making night hideous, frightening quiet folk out of their lives. Why don't you go to bed early, as I do? I never prowl round the oyster-bed, fighting other gentlemen oysters, making love to lady oysters already married. I never kill antelopes or missionaries. Why can't you live as I do on salt water and germs, or whatever it is that I do live on? Why don't you try to be more like me?"

An oyster has no evil passions, therefore we say he is a virtuous fish. We never ask ourselves – "Has he any good passions?" A lion's behaviour is often such as no just man could condone. Has he not his good points also?

Will the fat, sleek, "virtuous" man be as welcome at the gate of heaven as he supposes?

"Well," St. Peter may say to him, opening the door a little way and looking him up and down, "what is it now?"

"It's me." the virtuous man will reply, with an oily, self-satisfied smile; "I should say, I – I've come."

"Yes, I see you have come; but what is your claim to admittance? What have you done with your three score years and ten?"

"Done!" the virtuous man will answer, "I have done nothing, I assure you."

"Nothing!"

"Nothing; that is my strong point; that is why I am here. I have never done any wrong."

"And what good have you done?"

"What good!"

"Aye, what good? Do not you even know the meaning of the word? What human creature is the better for your having eaten and drunk and slept these years? You have done no harm – no harm to yourself. Perhaps, if you had you might have done some good with it; the two are generally to be found together down below, I remember. What good have you done that you should enter here? This is no mummy chamber; this is the place of men and women who have lived, who have wrought good – and evil also, alas! – for the sinners who fight for the right, not the righteous who run with their souls from the fight."

It was not, however, to speak of these things that I remembered *The Amateur* and its lessons. My intention was but to lead up to the story of a certain small boy, who in the doing of tasks not required of him was exceedingly clever. I wish to tell you his story, because, as do most true tales, it possesses a moral, and stories without a moral I deem to be but foolish literature, resembling roads that lead to nowhere, such as sick folk tramp for exercise.

I have known this little boy to take an expensive eight-day clock to pieces, and make of it a toy steamboat. True, it was not, when made, very much of a steamboat; but taking into consideration all the difficulties – the inadaptability of eight-day clock machinery to steamboat requirements, the necessity of getting the work accomplished quickly, before conservatively-minded people with no enthusiasm for science could interfere – a good enough steamboat. With merely an ironing-board and a few dozen meat-skewers, he would – provided the ironing-board was not missed in time – turn out quite a practicable rabbit-hutch. He could make a gun out of an umbrella and a gas-bracket, which, if not so accurate as a Martini-Henry, was, at all events, more deadly. With half the garden-hose, a copper scalding-pan out of the dairy, and a few Dresden china ornaments off the drawing-room mantelpiece, he would build a fountain for the garden. He could make book-shelves out of kitchen tables, and cross-bows out of crinolines. He could dam you a stream so that all the water would flow over the croquet lawn. He knew how to make red paint and oxygen gas, together with many other such-like commodities handy to have about a house. Among other things he learned how to make fireworks, and after a few explosions of an unimportant character, came to make them very well indeed. The boy who can play a good game of cricket is liked. The boy who can fight well is respected. The boy who can cheek a master is loved. But the boy who can make fireworks is revered above all others as a boy belonging to a superior order of beings. The fifth of November was at hand, and with the consent of an indulgent mother, he determined to give to the world a proof of his powers. A large party of friends, relatives, and school-mates was invited, and for a fortnight beforehand the scullery was converted into a manufactory for fireworks. The female servants went about in hourly terror of their lives, and the villa, did we judge exclusively by smell, one might have imagined had been taken over by Satan, his main premises being inconveniently crowded, as an annex. By the evening of the fourth all was in readiness, and samples were tested to make sure that no *contretemps* should occur the following night. All was found to be perfect. The rockets rushed heavenward and descended in stars, the Roman candles tossed their fiery balls into the darkness, the Catherine wheels sparkled and whirled, the crackers cracked, and the squibs banged. That night he went to bed a proud and happy boy, and dreamed of fame. He stood surrounded by blazing fireworks, and the vast crowd cheered him. His relations, most of whom, he knew, regarded him as the coming idiot of the family, were there to witness his triumph; so too was Dickey Bowles, who laughed at him because he could not throw straight. The girl at the bun-shop, she also was there, and saw that he was clever.

The night of the festival arrived, and with it the guests. They sat, wrapped up in shawls and cloaks, outside the hall door – uncles, cousins, aunts, little boys and big boys, little girls and big girls, with, as the theatre posters say, villagers and retainers, some forty of them in all, and waited.

But the fireworks did not go off. Why they did not go off I cannot explain; nobody ever *could* explain. The laws of nature seemed to be suspended for that night only. The rockets fell down and died where they stood. No human agency seemed able to ignite the squibs. The crackers gave one bang and collapsed. The Roman candles might have been English rushlights. The Catherine wheels became mere revolving glow-worms. The fiery serpents could not collect among them the spirit of a tortoise. The set piece, a ship at sea, showed one mast and the captain, and then went out. One or two items did their duty, but this only served to render the foolishness of the whole more striking. The little girls giggled, the little boys chaffed, the aunts and cousins said it was beautiful, the uncles inquired if it was all over, and talked about supper and trains, the "villagers and retainers" dispersed laughing, the indulgent mother said "never mind," and explained how well everything had gone off yesterday; the clever little boy crept upstairs to his room, and blubbered his heart out in the dark.

Hours later, when the crowd had forgotten him, he stole out again into the garden. He sat down amid the ruins of his hope, and wondered what could have caused the fiasco. Still puzzled, he drew from his pocket a box of matches, and, lighting one, he held it to the seared end of a rocket he had tried in vain to light four hours ago. It smouldered for an instant, then shot with a swish into the air and broke into a hundred points of fire. He tried another and another with the same result. He made a fresh attempt to fire the set piece. Point by point the whole picture – minus the captain and one mast – came out of the night, and stood revealed in all the majesty of flame. Its sparks fell upon the piled-up heap of candles, wheels, and rockets that a little while before had obstinately refused to burn, and that, one after another, had been thrown aside as useless. Now with the night frost upon them, they leaped to light in one grand volcanic eruption. And in front of the gorgeous spectacle he stood with only one consolation – his mother's hand in his.

The whole thing was a mystery to him at the time, but, as he learned to know life better, he came to understand that it was only one example of a solid but inexplicable fact, ruling all human affairs – *your fireworks won't go off while the crowd is around*.

Our brilliant repartees do not occur to us till the door is closed upon us and we are alone in the street, or, as the French would say, are coming down the stairs. Our after-dinner oratory, that sounded so telling as we delivered it before the looking-glass, falls strangely flat amidst the clinking of the glasses. The passionate torrent of words we meant to pour into her ear becomes a halting rigmarole, at which – small blame to her – she only laughs.

I would, gentle Reader, you could hear the stories that I meant to tell you. You judge me, of course, by the stories of mine that you have read – by this sort of thing, perhaps; but that is not just to me. The stories I have *not* told you, that I am going to tell you one day, I would that you judge me by those. They are so beautiful; you will say so; over them, you will laugh and cry with me.

They come into my brain unbidden, they clamour to be written, yet when I take my pen in hand they are gone. It is as though they were shy of publicity, as though they would say to me – "You alone, you shall read us, but you must not write us; we are too real, too true. We are like the thoughts you cannot speak. Perhaps a little later, when you know more of life, then you shall tell us."

Next to these in merit I would place, were I writing a critical essay on myself, the stories I have begun to write and that remain unfinished, why I cannot explain to myself. They are good stories, most of them; better far than the stories I have accomplished. Another time, perhaps, if you care to listen, I will tell you the beginning of one or two and you shall judge. Strangely enough, for I have always regarded myself as a practical, common-sensed man, so many of these still-born children of my mind I find, on looking through the cupboard where their thin bodies lie, are ghost stories. I suppose the hope of ghosts is with us all. The world grows somewhat interesting to us heirs of all the ages. Year by year, Science with broom and duster tears down the moth-worn tapestry, forces the doors of the locked chambers, lets light into the secret stairways, cleans out the dungeons, explores the hidden passages – finding every-where only dust. This echoing old castle, the world, so full of mystery in the days when we were children, is losing somewhat its charm for us as we grow older. The king sleeps no longer in the hollow of the hills. We have tunnelled through his mountain chamber. We have shivered his beard with our pick. We have driven the gods from Olympus. No wanderer through the moonlit groves now fears or hopes the sweet, death-giving gleam of Aphrodite's face. Thor's hammer echoes not among the peaks – 'tis but the thunder of the excursion train. We have swept the woods of the fairies. We have filtered the sea of its nymphs. Even the ghosts are leaving us, chased by the Psychical Research Society.

Perhaps of all, they are the least, however, to be regretted. They were dull old fellows, clanking their rusty chains and groaning and sighing. Let them go.

And yet how interesting they might be, if only they would. The old gentleman in the coat of mail, who lived in King John's reign, who was murdered, so they say, on the outskirts of the very wood I can see from my window as I write – stabbed in the back, poor gentleman, as he was riding home, his body flung into the moat that to this day is called Tor's tomb. Dry enough it is now, and the primroses love its steep banks; but a gloomy enough place in those days, no doubt, with its twenty feet of stagnant water. Why does he haunt the forest paths at night, as they tell me he does, frightening the children out of their wits, blanching the faces and stilling the laughter of the peasant lads and lasses, slouching home from the village dance? Instead, why does he not come up here and talk to me? He should have my easy-chair and welcome, would he only be cheerful and companianable. What brave tales could he not tell me. He fought in the first Crusade, heard the clarion voice of Peter, met the great Godfrey face to face, stood, hand on sword-hilt, at Runny-mede, perhaps. Better than a whole library of historical novels would an evening's chat be with such a ghost. What has he done with his eight hundred years of death? where has he been? what has he seen? Maybe he has visited Mars; has spoken to the strange spirits who can live in the liquid fires of Jupiter. What has he learned of the great secret? Has he found the truth? or is he, even as I, a wanderer still seeking the unknown?

You, poor, pale, grey nun – they tell me that of midnights one may see your white face peering from the ruined belfry window, hear the clash of sword and shield among the cedar-trees beneath.

It was very sad, I quite understand, my dear lady. Your lovers both were killed, and you retired to a convent. Believe me, I am sincerely sorry for you, but why waste every night renewing the whole painful experience? Would it not be better forgotten? Good Heavens, madam, suppose we living folk were to spend our lives wailing and wringing our hands because of the wrongs done to us when we were children? It is all over now. Had he lived, and had you married him, you might not have been happy. I do not wish to say anything unkind, but marriages founded upon the sincerest mutual love have sometimes turned out unfortunately, as you must surely know.

Do take my advice. Talk the matter over with the young men themselves. Persuade them to shake hands and be friends. Come in, all of you, out of the cold, and let us have some reasonable talk.

Why seek you to trouble us, you poor pale ghosts? Are we not your children? Be our wise friends. Tell me, how loved the young men in your young days? how answered the maidens? Has the world changed much, do you think? Had you not new women even then? girls who hated the everlasting tapestry frame and spinning-wheel? Your father's servants, were they so much worse off than the freemen who live in our East-end slums and sew slippers for fourteen hours a day at a wage of nine shillings a week? Do you think Society much improved during the last thousand years? Is it worse? is it better? or is it, on the whole, about the same, save that we call things by other names? Tell me, what have *you* learned?

Yet might not familiarity breed contempt, even for ghosts.

One has had a tiring day's shooting. One is looking forward to one's bed. As one opens the door, however, a ghostly laugh comes from behind the bed-curtains, and one groans inwardly, knowing what is in store for one: a two or three hours' talk with rowdy old Sir Lanval – he of the lance. We know all his tales by heart, and he will shout them. Suppose our aunt, from whom we have expectations, and who sleeps in the next room, should wake and overhear! They were fit and proper enough stories, no doubt, for the Round Table, but we feel sure our aunt would not appreciate them: – that story about

Sir Agravain and the cooper's wife! and he always will tell that story.

Or imagine the maid entering after dinner to say –

"Oh, if you please, sir, here is the veiled lady."

"What, again!" says your wife, looking up from her work.

"Yes, ma'am; shall I show her up into the bedroom?"

"You had better ask your master," is the reply. The tone is suggestive of an unpleasant five minutes so soon as the girl shall have withdrawn, but what are you to do?

"Yes, yes, show her up," you say, and the girl goes out, closing the door.

Your wife gathers her work together, and rises.

"Where are you going?" you ask.

"To sleep with the children," is the frigid answer.

"It will look so rude," you urge. "We must be civil to the poor thing; and you see it really is her room, as one might say. She has always haunted it."

"It is very curious," returns the wife of your bosom, still more icily, "that she never haunts it except when you are down here. Where she goes when you are in town I'm sure I don't know."

This is unjust. You cannot restrain your indignation.

"What nonsense you talk, Elizabeth," you reply; "I am only barely polite to her."

"Some men have such curious notions of politeness," returns Elizabeth. "But pray do not let us quarrel. I am only anxious not to disturb you. Two are company, you know. I don't choose to be the third, that's all." With which she goes out.

And the veiled lady is still waiting for you up-stairs. You wonder how long she will stop, also what will happen after she is gone.

I fear there is no room for you, ghosts, in this our world. You remember how they came to Hiawatha – the ghosts of the departed loved ones. He had prayed to them that they would come back to him to comfort him, so one day they crept into his wigwam, sat in silence round his fireside, chilled the air for Hiawatha, froze the smiles of Laughing Water.

There is no room for you, oh you poor, pale ghosts, in this our world. Do not trouble us. Let us forget. You, stout elderly matron, your thin locks turning grey, your eyes grown weak, your chin more ample, your voice harsh with much scolding and complaining, needful, alas! to household management, I pray you leave me. I loved you while you lived. How sweet, how beautiful you were. I see you now in your white frock among the apple-blossom. But you are dead, and your ghost disturbs my dreams. I would it haunted me not.

You, dull old fellow, looking out at me from the glass at which I shave, why do you haunt me? You are the ghost of a bright lad I once knew well. He might have done much, had he lived. I always had faith in him. Why do you haunt me? I would rather think of him as I remember him. I never imagined he would make such a poor ghost.

ON THE PREPARATION AND EMPLOYMENT OF LOVE PHILTRES

Occasionally a friend will ask me some such question as this, Do you prefer dark women or fair? Another will say, Do you like tall women or short? A third, Do you think light-hearted women, or serious, the more agreeable company? I find myself in the position that, once upon a time, overtook a certain charming young lady of taste who was asked by an anxious parent, the years mounting, and the family expenditure not decreasing, which of the numerous and eligible young men, then paying court to her, she liked the best. She replied, that was her difficulty. She could not make up her mind which she liked the best. They were all so nice. She could not possible select one to the exclusion of all the others. What she would have liked would have been to marry the lot, but that, she presumed, was impracticable.

I feel I resemble that young lady, not so much, perhaps, in charm and beauty as indecision of mind, when questions such as the above are put to me. It is as if one were asked one's favourite food. There are times when one fancies an egg with one's tea. On other occasions one dreams of a kipper. To-day one clamours for lobsters. To-morrow one feels one never wishes to see a lobster again; one determines to settle down, for a time, to a diet of bread and milk and rice-pudding.

Asked suddenly to say whether I preferred ices to soup, or beefsteaks to caviare, I should be nonplussed.

I like tall women and short, dark women and fair, merry women and grave.

Do not blame me, Ladies, the fault lies with you. Every right-thinking man is an universal lover; how could it be otherwise? You are so diverse, yet each so charming of your kind; and a man's heart is large. You have no idea, fair Reader, how large a man's heart is: that is his trouble – sometimes yours.

May I not admire the daring tulip, because I love also the modest lily? May I not press a kiss upon the sweet violet, because the scent of the queenly rose is precious to me?

"Certainly not," I hear the Rose reply. "If you can see anything in her, you shall have nothing to do with me."

"If you care for that bold creature," says the Lily, trembling, "you are not the man I took you for. Good-bye."

"Go to your baby-faced Violet," cries the Tulip, with a toss of her haughty head. "You are just fitted for each other."

And then I return to the Lily, she tells me that she cannot trust me. She has watched me with those others. She knows me for a gad-about. Her gentle face is full of pain.

So I must live unloved merely because I love too much.

My wonder is that young men ever marry. The difficulty of selection must be appalling. I walked the other evening in Hyde Park. The band of the Life Guards played heart-lifting music, and the vast crowd were basking in a sweet enjoyment such as rarely woos the English toiler. I strolled among them, and my attention was chiefly drawn towards the women. The great majority of them were, I suppose, shop-girls, milliners, and others belonging to the lower middle-class. They had put on their best frocks, their bonniest hats, their newest gloves. They sat or walked in twos and threes, chattering and preening, as happy as young sparrows on a clothes line. And what a handsome crowd they made! I have seen German crowds, I have seen French crowds, I have seen Italian crowds; but nowhere do you find such a proportion of pretty women as among the English middle-class. Three women out of every four were worth looking at, every other woman was pretty, while every fourth, one might say without exaggeration, was beautiful. As I passed to and fro the idea occurred to me: suppose I were an unprejudiced young bachelor, free from predilection, looking for a wife; and let me suppose – it is only a fancy – that all these girls were ready and willing to accept me. I have only to choose! I grew bewildered. There were fair girls, to look at whom was fatal; dark girls that set one's heart aflame; girls with red gold hair and grave grey eyes, whom one would follow to the confines of the universe; baby-faced girls that one longed to love and cherish; girls with noble faces, whom a man might worship; laughing girls, with whom one could dance through life gaily; serious girls, with whom life would be sweet and good; domestic-looking girls – one felt such would make delightful wives; they would cook, and sew, and make of home a pleasant, peaceful place. Then wicked-looking girls came by, at the stab of whose bold eyes all orthodox thoughts were put to a flight, whose laughter turned the world into a mad carnival; girls one could mould; girls from whom one could learn; sad girls one wanted to comfort; merry girls who would cheer one; little girls, big girls, queenly girls, fairy-like girls.

Suppose a young man had to select his wife in this fashion from some twenty or thirty thousand; or that a girl were suddenly confronted with eighteen thousand eligible young bachelors, and told to take the one she wanted and be quick about it? Neither boy nor girl would ever marry. Fate is kinder to us. She understands, and assists us. In the hall of a Paris hotel I once overheard one lady asking another to recommend her a milliner's shop.

"Go to the Maison Nouvelle," advised the questioned lady, with enthusiasm. "They have the largest selection there of any place in Paris."

"I know they have," replied the first lady, "that is just why I don't mean to go there. It confuses me. If I see six bonnets I can tell the one I want in five minutes. If I see six hundred I come away without any bonnet at all. Don't you know a little shop?"

Fate takes the young man or the young woman aside.

"Come into this village, my dear," says Fate; "into this by-street of this salubrious suburb, into this social circle, into this church, into this chapel. Now, my dear boy, out of these seventeen young ladies, which will you have? — out of these thirteen young men, which would you like for your very own, my dear?"

"No, miss, I am sorry, but I am not able to show you our up-stairs department to-day, the lift is not working. But I am sure we shall be able to find something in this room to suit you. Just look round, my dear, perhaps you will see something."

"No, sir, I cannot show you the stock in the next room, we never take that out except for our very special customers. We keep our most expensive goods in that room. (Draw that curtain, Miss Circumstance, please. I have told you of that before.) Now, sir, wouldn't you like this one? This colour is quite the rage this season; we are getting rid of quite a lot of these."

"No, sir! Well, of course, it would not do for every one's taste to be the same. Perhaps something dark would suit you better. Bring out those two brunettes, Miss Circumstance. Charming girls both of them, don't you think so, sir? I should say the taller one for you, sir. Just one moment, sir, allow me. Now, what do you think of that, sir? might have been made to fit you, I'm sure. *You prefer the shorter one*. Certainly, sir, no difference to us at all. Both are the same price. There's nothing like having one's own fancy, I always say. *No*, sir, I cannot put her aside for you, we never do that. Indeed, there's rather a run on brunettes just at present. I had a gentleman in only this morning, looking at this particular one, and he is going to call again to-night. Indeed, I am not at all sure – Oh, of course, sir, if you like to settle on this one now, that ends the matter. (Put those others away, Miss Circumstance, please, and mark this one sold.) I feel sure you'll like her, sir, when you get her home. Thank *you*, sir. Good-morning!"

"Now, miss, have *you* see anything you fancy? *Yes*, miss, this is all we have at anything near your price. (Shut those other cupboards, Miss Circumstance; never show more stock than you are obliged to, it only confuses customers. How often am I to tell you that?) *Yes*, miss, you are quite right, there *is* a slight blemish. They all have some slight flaw. The makers say they can't help it – it's in the material. It's not once in a season we get a perfect specimen; and when we do ladies don't seem to care for it. Most of our customers prefer a little faultiness. They say it gives character. Now, look at this, miss. This sort of thing wears very well, warm and quiet. *You'd like one with more colour in it*? Certainly. Miss Circumstance, reach me down the art patterns. *No*, miss, we don't guarantee any of them over the year, so much depends on how you use them. *Oh yes*, miss, they'll stand a fair amount of wear. People do tell you the quieter patterns last longer; but my experience is that one is much the same as another. There's really no telling any of them until you come to try them. We never recommend one more than another. There's a lot of chance about these goods, it's in the nature of them. What I always say to ladies is – 'Please yourself, it's you who have got to wear it; and it's no good having an article you start by not liking.' *Yes*, miss, it *is* pretty and it looks well against you: it does indeed. Thank you, miss. Put that one aside, Miss Circumstance, please. See that it doesn't get mixed up with the unsold stock."

It is a useful philtre, the juice of that small western flower, that Oberon drops upon our eyelids as we sleep. It solves all difficulties in a trice. Why of course Helena is the fairer. Compare her with Hermia! Compare the raven with the dove! How could we ever have doubted for a moment? Bottom is an angel, Bottom is as wise as he is handsome. Oh, Oberon, we thank you for that drug. Matilda Jane is a goddess; Matilda Jane is a queen; no woman ever born of Eve was like Maltida Jane. The little pimple on her nose – her little, sweet, tip-tilted nose – how beautiful it is. Her bright eyes flash with temper now and then; how piquant is a temper in a woman. William is a dear old stupid, how lovable stupid men can be – especially when wise enough to love us. William does not shine in conversation; how we hate a magpie of a man. William's chin is what is called receding, just the sort of chin a beard looks well on. Bless you, Oberon darling, for that drug; rub it on our eyelids once again. Better let us have a bottle, Oberon, to keep by us.

Oberon, Oberon, what are you thinking of? You have given the bottle to Puck. Take it away from him, quick. Lord help us all if that Imp has the bottle. Lord save us from Puck while we sleep.

Or may we, fairy Oberon, regard your lotion as an eye-opener, rather than as an eye-closer? You remember the story the storks told the children, of the little girl who was a toad by day, only her sweet dark eyes being left to her. But at night, when the Prince clasped her close to his breast, lo! again she became the king's daughter, fairest and fondest of women. There be many royal ladies in Marshland, with bad complexion and this straight hair, and the silly princes sneer and ride away to woo some kitchen wench decked out in queen's apparel. Lucky the prince upon whose eyelids Oberon has dropped the magic philtre.

In the gallery of a minor Continental town I have forgotten, hangs a picture that lives with me. The painting I cannot recall, whether good or bad; artists must forgive me for remembering only the subject. It shows a man, crucified by the roadside. No martyr he. If ever a man deserved hanging it was this one. So much the artist has made clear. The face, even under its mask of agony, is an evil, treacherous face. A peasant girl clings to the cross; she stands tip-toe upon a patient donkey, straining her face upward for the half-dead man to stoop and kiss her lips.

Thief coward blackguard, they are stamped upon his face, but *under* the face, under the evil outside? Is there no remnant of manhood – nothing tender, nothing true? A woman has crept to the cross to kiss him: no evidence in his favour, my Lord? Love is blind – aye, to our faults. Heaven help us all; Love's eyes would be sore indeed if it were not so. But for the good that is in us her eyes are keen. You, crucified blackguard, stand forth. A hundred witnesses have given their evidence against you. Are there none to give evidence for him? A woman, great Judge, who loved him. Let her speak.

But I am wandering far from Hyde Park and its show of girls.

They passed and re-passed me, laughing, smiling, talking. Their eyes were bright with merry thoughts; their voices soft and musical. They were pleased, and they wanted to please. Some were married, some had evidently reasonable expectations of being married; the rest hoped to be. And we, myself, and some ten thousand other young men. I repeat it – myself and some ten thousand other young men; for who among us ever thinks of himself but as a young man? It is the world that ages, not we. The children cease their playing and grow grave, the lasses' eyes are dimmer. The hills are a little steeper, the milestones, surely, further apart. The songs the young men sing are less merry than the songs we used to sing. The days have grown a little colder, the wind a little keener. The wine has lost its flavour somewhat; the new humour is not like the old. The other boys are becoming dull and prosy; but *we* are not changed. It is the world that is growing old. Therefore, I brave your thoughtless laughter, youthful Reader, and repeat that we, myself and some ten thousand other young men, walked among these sweet girls; and, using our boyish eyes, fascinated, charmed, and captivated. How delightful to spend our lives with them, to do little services for them that would call up these bright smiles. How pleasant to jest with them, and hear their flute-like laughter, to console them and read their grateful eyes. Really life is a pleasant thing, and the idea of marriage undoubtedly originated in the brain of a kindly Providence.

We smiled back at them, and we made way for them; we rose from our chairs with a polite, "Allow me, miss," "Don't mention it, I prefer standing." "It is a delightful evening, is it not?" And perhaps – for what harm was there? – we dropped into conversation with these chance fellow-passengers upon the stream of life. There were those among us – bold daring spririts – who even went to the length of mild flirtation. Some of us knew some of them, and in such happy case there followed interchange of pretty pleasantries. Your English middle-class young man and woman are not adepts at the game of flirtation. I will confess that our methods were, perhaps, elephantine, that we may have grown a trifle noisy as the evening wore on. But we meant no evil; we did but our best to enjoy ourselves, to give enjoyment, to make the too brief time pass gaily.

And then my thoughts travelled to small homes in distant suburbs, and these bright lads and lasses round me came to look older and more careworn. But what of that? Are not old faces sweet when looked at by old eyes a little dimmed by love, and are not care and toil but the parents of peace and joy?

But as I drew nearer, I saw that many of the faces were seared with sour and angry looks, and the voices that rose round me sounded surly and captious. The pretty compliment and praise had changed to sneers and scoldings. The dimpled smile had wrinkled to a frown. There seemed so little desire to please, so great a determination not to be pleased.

And the flirtations! Ah me, they had forgotten how to flirt! Oh, the pity of it! All the jests were bitter, all the little services were given grudgingly. The air seemed to have grown chilly. A darkness had come over all things.

And then I awoke to reality, and found I had been sitting in my chair longer than I had intended. The band-stand was empty, the sun had set; I rose and made my way home through the scattered crowd.

Nature is so callous. The Dame irritates one at times by her devotion to her one idea, the propagation of the species.

"Multiply and be fruitful; let my world be ever more and more peopled."

For this she trains and fashions her young girls, models them with cunning hand, paints them with her wonderful red and white, crowns them with her glorious hair, teaches them to smile and laugh, trains their voices into music, sends them out into the world to captivate, to enslave us.

"See how beautiful she is, my lad," says the cunning old woman. "Take her; build your little nest with her in your pretty suburb; work for her and live for her; enable her to keep the little ones that I will send."

And to her, old hundred-breasted Artemis whispers, "Is he not a bonny lad? See how he loves you, how devoted he is to you! He will work for you and make you happy; he will build your home for you. You will be the mother of his children."

So we take each other by the hand, full of hope and love, and from that hour Mother Nature has done with us. Let the wrinkles come; let our voices grow harsh; let the fire she lighted in our hearts die out; let the foolish selfishness we both thought we had put behind us for ever creep back to us, bringing unkindness and indifference, angry thoughts and cruel words into our lives. What cares she? She has caught us, and chained us to her work. She is our universal mother-in-law. She has done the match-making; for the rest, she leaves it to ourselves. We can love or we can fight; it is all one to her, confound her.

I wonder sometimes if good temper might not be taught. In business we use no harsh language, say no unkind things to one another. The shopkeeper, leaning across the counter, is all smiles and affability, he might put up his shutters were he otherwise. The commercial gent, no doubt, thinks the ponderous shopwalker an ass, but refrains from telling him so. Hasty tempers are banished from the City. Can we not see that it is just as much to our interest to banish them from Tooting and Hampstead?

The young man who sat in the chair next to me, how carefully he wrapped the cloak round the shoulders of the little milliner beside him. And when she said she was tired of sitting still, how readily he sprang from his chair to walk with her, though it was evident he was very comfortable where he was. And she! She had laughed at his jokes; they were not very clever jokes, they were not very new. She had probably read them herself months before in her own particular weekly journal. Yet the harmless humbug made him happy. I wonder if ten years hence she will laugh at such old humour, if ten years hence he will take such clumsy pains to put her cape about her. Experience shakes her head, and is amused at my question.

I would have evening classes for the teaching of temper to married couples, only I fear the institution would languish for lack of pupils. The husbands would recommend their wives to attend, generously offering to pay the fee as a birthday present. The wife would be indignant at the suggestion of good money being thus wasted. "No, John, dear," she would unselfishly reply, "you need the lessons more than I do. It would be a shame for me to take them away from you," and they would wrangle upon the subject for the rest of the day.

Oh! the folly of it. We pack our hamper for life's picnic with such pains. We spend so much, we work so hard. We make choice pies, we cook prime joints, we prepare so carefully the mayonnaise, we mix with loving hands the salad, we cram the basket to the lid with every delicacy we can think of. Everything to make the picnic a success is there – except the salt. Ah! woe is me, we forget the salt. We slave at our desks, in our workshops, to make a home for those we love; we give up our pleasures, we give up our rest. We toil in our kitchen from morning till night, and we render the whole feast tasteless for want of a ha'porth of salt – for want of a *soupçon* of amiability, for want of a handful of kindly words, a touch of caresss, a pinch of courtesy.

Who does not know that estimable housewife, working from eight till twelve to keep the house in what she calls order? She is so good a woman, so untiring, so unselfish, so conscientious, so irritating. Her rooms are so clean, her servants so well managed, her children so well dressed, her dinners so well cooked; the whole house so uninviting. Everything about her is in apple-pie order, and everybody wretched.

My good Madam, you polish your tables, you scour your kettles, but the most valuable piece of furniture in the whole house you are letting go to rack and ruin for want of a little pains. You will find it in your own room, my dear Lady, in front of your own mirror. It is getting shabby and dingy, old-looking before its time; the polish is rubbed off it, Madam, it is losing its brightness and charm. Do you remember when he first brought it home, how proud he was of it? Do you think you have used it well, knowing how he valued it? A little less care of your pots and your pans, Madam, a little more of yourself were wiser. Polish yourself up, Madam; you had a pretty wit once, a pleasant laugh, a conversation that was not confined exclusively to the short-comings of servants, the wrong-doings of tradesmen. My dear Madam, we do not live on spotless linen, and crumbless carpets. Hunt out that bundle of old letters you keep tied up in faded ribbon at the back of your bureau drawer – a pity you don't read them oftener. He did not enthuse about your cuffs and collars, gush over the neatness of your darning. It was your tangled hair he raved about, your sunny smile (we have not seen it for some years, Madam – the fault of the Cook and the Butcher, I presume), your little hands, your rosebud mouth – it has lost its shape, Madam, of late. Try a little less scolding of Mary Ann, and practise a laugh once a day: you might get back the dainty curves. It would be worth trying. It was a pretty mouth once.

Who invented that mischievous falsehood that the way to a man's heart was through his stomach? How many a silly woman, taking it for truth, has let love slip out of the parlour, while she was busy in the kitchen. Of course, if you were foolish enough to marry a pig, I suppose you must be content to devote your life to the preparation of hog's-wash. But are you sure that he *is* a pig? If by any chance he be not? – then, Madam, you are making a grievous mistake. My dear Lady, you are too modest. If I may say so without making you unduly conceited, even at the dinner-table itself, you are of much more importance than the mutton. Courage, Madam, be not afraid to tilt a lance even with your own cook. You can be more piquant than the sauce *à la Tartare*, more soothing surely than the melted butter. There was a time when he would not have known whether he was eating beef or pork with you the other side of the table. Whose fault is it? Don't think so poorly of us. We are not ascetics, neither are we all gourmets: most of us plain men, fond of our dinner, as a healthy man should be, but fonder still of our sweethearts and wives, let us hope. Try us. A moderately-cooked dinner – let us even say a not-too-well-cooked dinner, with you looking your best, laughing and talking gaily and cleverly – as you can, you know – makes a pleasanter meal for us, after the day's work is done, than that same dinner, cooked to perfection, with you silent, jaded, and anxious, your pretty hair untidy, your pretty face wrinkled with care concerning the sole, with anxiety regarding the omelette.

My poor Martha, be not troubled about so many things. *You* are the one thing needful – if the bricks and mortar are to be a home. See to it that *you* are well served up, that *you* are done to perfection, that *you* are tender and satisfying, that *you* are worth sitting down to. We wanted a wife, a comrade, a friend; not a cook and a nurse on the cheap.

But of what use is it to talk? the world will ever follow its own folly. When I think of all the good advice that I have given it, and of the small result achieved, I confess I grow discouraged. I was giving good advice to a lady only the other day. I was instructing her as to the proper treatment of aunts. She was sucking a lead-pencil, a thing I am always telling her not to do. She took it out of her mouth to speak.

"I suppose you know how everybody ought to do everything," she said.

There are times when it is necessary to sacrifice one's modesty to one's duty.

"Of course I do," I replied.

"And does Mama know how everybody ought to do everything?" was the second question.

My conviction on this point was by no means so strong, but for domestic reasons I again sacrificed myself to expediency.

"Certainly," I answered; "and take that pencil out of your mouth. I've told you of that before. You'll swallow it one day, and then you'll get perichondritis and die."

She appeared to be solving a problem.

"All grown-up people seem to know everything," she summarized.

There are times when I doubt if children are as simple as they look. If it be sheer stupidity that prompts them to make remarks of this character, one should pity them, and seek to improve them. But if it be not stupidity? well then, one should still seek to improve them, but by a different method.

The other morning I overheard the nurse talking to this particular specimen. The woman is a most worthy creature, and she was imparting to the child some really sound advice. She was in the middle of an unexceptional exhortation concerning the virtue of silence, when Dorothea interrupted her with –

"Oh, do be quiet, Nurse. I never get a moment's peace from your chatter."

Such an interruption discourages a woman who is trying to do her duty.

Last Tuesday evening she was unhappy. Myself, I think that rhubarb should never be eaten before April, and then never with lemonade. Her mother read her a homily upon the subject of pain. It was impressed upon her that we must be patient, that we must put up with the trouble that God sends us. Dorothea would descend to details, as children will.

"Must we put up with the cod-liver oil that God sends us?"

"Yes, decidedly."

"And with the nurses that God sends us?"

"Certainly; and be thankful that you've got them, some little girls haven't any nurse. And don't talk so much."

On Friday I found the mother in tears.

"What's the matter?" I asked.

"Oh, nothing," was the answer; "only Baby. She's such a strange child. I can't make her out at all."

"What has she been up to now?"

"Oh, she will argue, you know."

She has that failing. I don't know where she gets it from, but she's got it.

"Well?"

"Well, she made me cross; and, to punish her, I told her she shouldn't take her doll's perambulator out with her."

"Yes?"

"Well, she didn't say anything then, but so soon as I was outside the door, I heard her talking to herself – you know her way?"

"Yes?"

"She said —"

"Yes, she said?"

"She said, 'I must be patient. I must put up with the mother God has sent me.'"

She lunches down-stairs on Sundays. We have her with us once a week to give her the opportunity of studying manners and behaviour. Milson had dropped in, and we were discussing politics. I was interested, and, pushing my plate aside, leant forward with my elbows on the table. Dorothea has a habit of talking to herself in a high-pitched whisper capable of being heard above an Adelphi love scene. I heard her say –

"I must sit up straight. I mustn't sprawl with my elbows on the table. It is only common, vulgar people behave that way."

I looked across at her; she was sitting most correctly, and appeared to be contemplating something a thousand miles away. We had all of us been lounging! We sat up stiffly, and conversation flagged.

Of course we made a joke of it after the child was gone. But somehow it didn't seem to be *our* joke.

I wish I could recollect my childhood. I should so like to know if children are as simple as they can look.

ON THE DELIGHTS AND BENEFITS
OF SLAVERY

My study window looks down upon Hyde Park, and often, to quote the familiar promise of each new magazine, it amuses and instructs me to watch from my tower the epitome of human life that passes to and fro beneath. At the opening of the gates, creeps in the woman of the streets. Her pitiful work for the time being is over. Shivering in the chill dawn, she passes to her brief rest. Poor Slave! Lured to the galley's lowest deck, then chained there. Civilization, tricked fool, they say has need of such. You serve as the dogs of Eastern towns. But at least, it seems to me, we need not spit on you. Home to your kennel! Perchance, if the Gods be kind, they may send you dreams of a cleanly hearth, where you lie with a silver collar round your neck.

Next comes the labourer – the hewer of wood, the drawer of water – slouching wearily to his toil; sleep clinging still about his leaden eyes, his pittance of food carried tied up in a dish-clout. The first stroke of the hour clangs from Big Ben. Haste thee, fellow-slave, lest the overseer's whip, "Out, we will have no lie-a-beds here," descend upon thy patient back.

Later, the artisan, with his bag of tools across his shoulder. He, too, listens fearfully to the chiming of the bells. For him also there hangs ready the whip.

After him, the shop boy and the shop girl, making love

as they walk, not to waste time. And after these the slaves of the desk and of the warehouse, employers and employed, clerks and tradesmen, office boys and merchants. To your places, slaves of all ranks. Get you unto your burdens.

Now, laughing and shouting as they run, the children, the sons and daughters of the slaves. Be industrious, little children, and learn your lessons, that when the time comes you may be ready to take from our hands the creaking oar, to slip into our seat at the roaring loom. For we shall not be slaves for ever, little children. It is the good law of the land. So many years in the galleys, so many years in the fields; then we can claim our freedom. Then we shall go, little children, back to the land of our birth. And you we must leave behind us to take up the tale of our work. So, off to your schools, little children, and learn to be good little slaves.

Next, pompous and sleek, come the educated slaves – journalists, doctors, judges, and poets; the attorney, the artist, the player, the priest. They likewise scurry across the Park, looking anxiously from time to time at their watches, lest they be late for their appointments; thinking of the rates and taxes to be earned, of the bonnets to be paid for, the bills to be met. The best scourged, perhaps, of all, these slaves. The cat reserved for them has fifty tails in place of merely two or three. Work, you higher middle-class slave, or you shall come down to the smoking of twopenny cigars; harder yet, or you shall drink shilling claret; harder, or you shall lose your carriage and ride in a penny bus; your wife's frocks shall be of last year's fashion; your trousers shall bag at the knees; from Kensington you shall be banished to Kilburn, if the tale of your bricks run short. Oh, a many-thonged whip is yours, my genteel brother.

The slaves of fashion are the next to pass beneath me in review. They are dressed and curled with infinite pains. The liveried, pampered footman these, kept more for show than use; but their senseless tasks none the less labour to them. Here must they come every day, merry or sad. By this gravel path and no other must they walk; these phrases shall they use when they speak to one another. For an hour they must go slowly up and down upon a bicycle from Hyde Park Corner to the Magazine and back. And these clothes must they wear; their gloves of this colour, their neckties of this pattern. In the afternoon they must return again, this time in a carriage, dressed in another livery, and for an hour they must pass slowly to and fro in foolish procession. For dinner they must don yet another livery, and after dinner they must stand about at dreary social functions till with weariness and boredom their heads feel dropping from their shoulders.

With the evening come the slaves back from their work: barristers, thinking out their eloquent appeals; school-boys, conning their dog-eared grammars; City men, planning their schemes; the wearers of motley, cudgelling their poor brains for fresh wit with which to please their master; shop boys and shop girls, silent now as, together, they plod homeward; the artisan; the labourer. Two or three hours you shall have to yourselves, slaves, to think and love and play, if you be not too tired to think, or love, or play. Then to your litter, that you may be ready for the morrow's task.

The twilight deepens into dark; there comes back the woman of the streets. As the shadows, she rounds the City's day. Work strikes its tent. Evil creeps from its peering place.

So we labour, driven by the whip of necessity, an army of slaves. If we do not our work, the whip descends upon us; only the pain we feel in our stomach instead of on our back. And because of that, we call ourselves free men.

Some few among us bravely struggle to be really free: they are our tramps and outcasts. We well-behaved slaves shrink from them, for the wages of freedom in this world are vermin and starvation. We can live lives worth living only by placing the collar round our neck.

There are times when one asks oneself: Why this endless labour? Why this building of houses, this cooking of food, this making of clothes? Is the ant so much more to be envied than the grasshopper, because she spends her life in grubbing and storing, and can spare no time for singing? Why this complex instinct, driving us to a thousand labours to satisfy a thousand desires? We have turned the world into a workshop to provide ourselves with toys. To purchase luxury we have sold our ease.

Oh, Children of Israel! why were ye not content in your wilderness? It seems to have been a pattern wilderness. For you, a simple wholesome food, ready cooked, was provided. You took no thought for rent and taxes; you had no poor among you – no poor-rate collectors. You suffered not from indigestion, nor the hundred ills that follow over-feeding; an omer for every man was your portion, neither more nor less. You knew not you had a liver. Doctors wearied you not with their theories, their physics, and their bills. You were neither landowners nor leaseholders, neither shareholders nor debenture holders. The weather and the market reports troubled you not. The lawyer was unknown to you; you wanted no advice; you had nought to quarrel about with your neighbour. No riches were yours for the moth and rust to damage. Your yearly income and expenditure you knew would balance to a fraction. Your wife and children were provided for. Your old age caused you no anxiety; you knew you could always have enough to live upon in comfort. Your funeral, a simple and tasteful affair, would be furnished by the tribe. And yet, poor, foolish child, fresh from the Egyptian brickfield, you could not rest satisfied. You hungered for the flesh-pots, knowing well what flesh-pots entail: the cleaning of the flesh-pots, the forging of the flesh-pots, the hewing of wood to make the fires for the boiling of the flesh-pots, the breeding of beasts to fill the pots, the growing of fodder to feed the beasts to fill the pots.

All the labour of our life is centred round our flesh-pots. On the altar of the flesh-pot we sacrifice our leisure, our peace of mind. For a mess of pottage we sell our birthright.

Oh! Children of Israel, saw you not the long punishment you were preparing for yourselves, when in your wilderness you set up the image of the Calf, and fell before it, crying – "This shall be our God."

You would have veal. Thought you never of the price man pays for Veal? The servants of the Golden Calf! I see them, stretched before my eyes, a weary, endless throng. I see them toiling in the mines, the black sweat on their faces. I see them in sunless cities, silent, and grimy, and bent. I see them, ague-twisted, in the rain-soaked fields. I see them, panting by the furnace doors. I see them, in loin-cloth and necklace, the load upon their head. I see them in blue coats and red coats, marching to pour their blood as an offering on the altar of the Calf. I see them in homespun and broadcloth, I see them in smock and gaiters, I see them in cap and apron, the servants of the Calf. They swarm on the land and they dot the sea. They are chained to the anvil and counter; they are chained to the bench and the desk. They make ready the soil, they till the fields where the Golden Calf is born. They build the ship, and they sail the ship that carries the Golden Calf. They fashion the pots, they mould the pans, they carve the tables, they turn the chairs, they dream of the sauces, they dig for the salt, they weave the damask, they mould the dish to serve the Golden Calf.

The work of the world is to this end, that we eat of the Calf. War and Commerce, Science and Law! what are they but the four pillars supporting the Golden Calf? He is our God. It is on his back that we have journeyed from the primeval forest, where our ancestors ate nuts and fruit. He is our God. His temple is in every street. His blue-robed priest stands ever at the door, calling to the people to worship. Hark! his voice rises on the gas-tainted air — "Now's your time! Now's your time! Buy! Buy! ye people. Bring hither the sweat of your brow, the sweat of your brain, the ache of your heart, buy Veal with it. Bring me the best years of your life. Bring me your thoughts, your hopes, your loves; ye shall have Veal for them. Now's your time! Now's your time! Buy! Buy!"

Oh! Children of Israel, was Veal, even with all its trimmings, quite worth the price?

And we! What wisdom have we learned, during the centuries? I talked with a rich man only the other evening. He calls himself a Financier, whatever that may mean. He leaves his beautiful house, some twenty miles out of London, at a quarter to eight, summer and winter, after a hurried breakfast by himself, while his guests still sleep, and he gets back just in time to dress for an elaborate dinner he himself is too weary or too preoccupied to more than touch. If ever he is persuaded to give himself a holiday it is for a fortnight in Ostend, when it is most crowded and uncomfortable. He takes his secretary with him, receives and despatches a hundred telegrams a day, and has a private telephone, through which he can speak direct to London, brought up into his bedroom.

I suppose the telephone is really a useful invention. Business men tell me they wonder how they contrived to conduct their affairs without it. My own wonder always is, how any human being with the ordinary passions of his race can conduct his business, or even himself, creditably, within a hundred yards of the invention. I can imagine Job, or Griselda, or Socrates liking to have a telephone about them as exercise. Socrates, in particular, would have made quite a reputation for himself out of a three months' subscription to a telephone. Myself, I am, perhaps, too sensitive. I once lived for a month in an office with a telephone, if one could call it life. I was told that if I had stuck to the thing for two or three months longer, I should have got used to it. I know friends of mine, men once fearless and high-spirited, who now stand in front of their own telephone for a quarter of an hour at a time, and never so much as answer it back. They tell me that at first they used to swear and shout at it as I did; but now their spirit seems crushed. That is what happens: you either break the telephone, or the telephone breaks you. You want to see a man two streets off. You might put on your hat, and be round at his office in five minutes. You are on the point of starting when the telephone catches your eye. You think you will ring him up to make sure he is in. You commence by ringing up some half-dozen times before anybody takes any notice of you whatever. You are burning with indignation at this neglect, and have left the instrument to sit down and pen a stinging letter of complaint to the Company when the ring-back re-calls you. You seize the ear trumpets, and shout –

"How is it that I can never get an answer when I ring? Here have I been ringing for the last half-hour. I have rung twenty times." (This is a falsehood. You have rung only six times, and the "half-hour" is an absurd exaggeration; but you feel the mere truth would not be adequate to the occasion.) "I think it disgraceful," you continue, "and I shall complain to the Company. What is the use of my having a telephone if I can't get any answer when I ring? Here I pay a large sum for having this thing, and I can't get any notice taken. I've been ringing all the morning. Why is it?"

Then you wait for the answer.

"What – what do you say? I can't hear what you say."

"I say I've been ringing here for over an hour, and I can't get any reply," you call back. "I shall complain to the Company."

"You want what? Don't stand so near the tube. I can't hear what you say. What number?"

"Bother the number; I say why is it I don't get an answer when I ring?"

"Eight hundred and what?"

You can't argue any more, after that. The machine would give way under the language you want to make use of. Half of what you feel would probably cause an explosion at some point where the wire was weak. Indeed, mere language of any kind would fall short of the requirements of the case. A hatchet and a gun are the only intermediaries through which you could convey your meaning by this time. So you give up all attempt to answer back, and meekly mention that you want to be put in communication with four-five-seven-six.

"Four-nine-seven-six?" says the girl.

"No, four-five-seven-six."

"Did you say seven-six or six-seven?"

"Six-seven – no! I mean seven-six: no – wait a minute. I don't know what I do mean now."

"Well, I wish you'd find out," says the young lady severely. "You are keeping me here all the morning."

So you look up the number in the book again, and at last she tells you that you are in connection; and then, ramming the trumpet tight against your ear, you stand waiting.

And if there is one thing more than another likely to make a man feel ridiculous it is standing on tip-toe in a corner, holding a machine to his head, and listening intently to nothing. Your back aches and your head aches, your very hair aches. You hear the door open behind you and somebody enter the room. You can't turn your head. You swear at them, and hear the door close with a bang. It immediately occurs to you that in all probability it was Henrietta. She promised to call for you at half-past twelve: you were to take her to lunch. It was twelve o'clock when you were fool enough to mix yourself up with this infernal machine, and it probably *is* half-past twelve by now. Your past life rises before you, accompanied by dim memories of your grandmother. You are wondering how much longer you can bear the strain of this attitude, and whether after all you do really want to see the man in the next street but two, when the girl in the exchange-room calls up to know if you're done.

"Done!" you retort bitterly; "why I haven't begun yet."

"Well, be quick," she says, "because you're wasting time."

Thus admonished, you attack the thing again. "*Are* you there?" you cry in tones that ought to move the heart of a Charity Commissioner; and then, oh joy! oh rapture! you hear a faint human voice replying –

"Yes, what is it?"

"Oh! Are you four-five-seven-six?"

"What?"

"Are you four-five-seven-six, Williamson?"

"What! who are you?"

"Eight-one-nine, Jones."

"Bones?"

"No, *Jones*. Are you four-five-seven-six?"

"Yes; what is it?"

"Is Mr. Williamson in?"

"Will I what – who are you?"

"Jones! Is Mr. Williamson in?"

"Who?"

"Williamson. Will-i-am-son!"

"You're the son of what? I can't hear what you say."

Then you gather yourself for one final effort, and succeed, by superhuman patience, in getting the fool to understand that you wish to know if Mr. Williamson is in, and he says, so it sounds to you, "Be in all the morning."

So you snatch up your hat and run round.

"Oh, I've come to see Mr. Williamson," you say.

"Very sorry, sir," is the polite reply, "but he's out."

"Out? Why, you just now told me through the telephone that he'd be in all the morning."

"No, I said, he '*won't*' be in all the morning.'"

You go back to the office, and sit down in front of that telephone and look at it. There it hangs, calm and imperturbable. Were it an ordinary instrument, that

would be its last hour. You would go straight down-
stairs, get the coal-hammer and the kitchen-poker, and
divide it into sufficient pieces to give a bit to every man
in London. But you feel nervous of these electrical
affairs, and there is a something about that telephone,
with its black hole and curly wires, that cows you. You
have a notion that if you don't handle it properly
something may come and shock you, and then there will
be an inquest, and bother of that sort, so you only curse
it.

That is what happens when you want to use the
telephone from your end. But that is not the worst that
the telephone can do. A sensible man, after a little
experience, can learn to leave the thing alone. Your worst
troubles are not of your own making. You are working
against time; you have given instructions not to be
disturbed. Perhaps it is after lunch, and you are thinking
with your eyes closed, so that your thoughts shall not be
distracted by the objects about the room. In either case
you are anxious not to leave your chair, when off goes
that telephone bell and you spring from your chair,
uncertain, for the moment, whether you have been shot,
or blown up with dynamite. It occurs to you in your
weakness that if you persist in taking no notice, they will
get tired, and leave you alone. But that is not their
method. The bell rings violently at ten-second intervals.
You have nothing to wrap your head up in. You think it
will be better to get this business over and done with.
You go to your fate and call back savagely –

"What is it? What do you want?"

No answer, only a confused murmur, prominent out of
which come the voices of two men swearing at one
another. The language they are making use of is
disgraceful. The telephone seems peculiarly adapted for
the conveyance of blasphemy. Ordinary language sounds
indistinct through it; but every word those two men are
saying can be heard by all the telephone subscribers in
London.

It is useless attempting to listen till they have done. When they are exhausted, you apply to the tube again. No answer is obtainable. You get mad, and become sarcastic; only being sarcastic when you are not sure that anybody is at the other end to hear you is unsatisfying.

At last, after a quarter of an hour or so of saying, "Are you there?" "Yes, I'm here," "Well?" the young lady at the Exchange asks what you want.

"I don't want anything," you reply.

"Then why do you keep talking?" she retorts; "you mustn't play with the thing."

This renders you speechless with indignation for a while, upon recovering from which you explain that somebody rang you up.

"*Who* rang you up?" she asks.

"I don't know."

"I wish you did," she observes.

Generally disgusted, you slam the trumpet up and return to your chair. The instant you are seated the bell clangs again; and you fly up and demand to know what the thunder they want, and who the thunder they are.

"Don't speak so loud, we can't hear you. What do you want?" is the answer.

"I don't want anything. What do *you* want? Why do you ring me up, and then not answer me? Do leave me alone, if you can."

"We can't get Hong Kong at seventy-four."

"Well, I don't care if you can't."

"Would you like Zulus?"

"What are you talking about?" you reply; "I don't know what you mean."

"Would you like Zulus – Zulus at seventy-three and a half?"

"I wouldn't have 'em at six a penny. What are you talking about?"

"Hong Kongs – we can't get them at seventy-four. Oh, half-a-minute" (the half-a-minute passes). "Are you there?"

"Yes, but you are talking to the wrong man."

"We can get you Hong Kong at seventy-four and seven-eights."

"Bother Hong Kongs, and you too. I tell you, you are talking to the wrong man. I've told you once."

"Once what?"

"Why, that I am the wrong man – I mean that you are talking to the wrong man."

"Who are you?"

"Eight-one-nine, Jones."

"Oh, aren't you one-nine-eight?"

"No."

"Oh, good-bye."

"Good-bye."

How can a man after that sit down and write pleasantly of the European crisis? And, if it were needed, herein lies another indictment against the telephone. I was engaged in an argument, which, if not in itself serious, was at least concerned with a serious enough subject, the unsatisfactory nature of human riches; and from that highly moral discussion have I been lured, by the accidental sight of the word "telephone," into the writing of matter which can have the effect only of exciting to frenzy all critics of the New Humour into whose hands, for their sins, this book may come. Let me forget my transgression and return to my sermon, or rather to the sermon of my millionaire acquaintance.

It was one day after dinner, we sat together in his magnificently furnished dining-room. We had lighted our cigars at the silver lamp. The butler had withdrawn.

"These cigars we are smoking," my friend suddenly remarked, *à propos* apparently of nothing, "they cost me five shillings apiece, taking them by the thousand."

"I can quite believe it," I answered; "they are worth it."

"Yes, to you," he replied, almost savagely. "What do you usually pay for your cigars?"

We had known each other years ago. When I first met him his offices consisted of a back room up three flights of stairs in a dingy by-street off the Strand, which has since disappeared. We occasionally dined together, in those days, at a restaurant in Great Portland Street, for one and nine. Our acquaintanceship was of sufficient standing to allow of such a question.

"Threepence," I answered. "They work out at about twopence three-farthings by the box."

"Just so," he growled; "and your two-penny-three-farthing weed gives you precisely the same amount of satisfaction that this five shilling cigar affords me. That means four and ninepence farthing wasted every time I smoke. I pay my cook two hundred a year. I don't enjoy my dinner as much as when it cost me four shillings, including a quarter flask of Chianti. What is the difference, personally, to me whether I drive to my office in a carriage and pair, or in an omnibus? I often do ride in a bus: it saves trouble. It is absurd wasting time looking for one's coachman, when the conductor of an omnibus that passes one's door is hailing one a few yards off. Before I could afford even buses – when I used to walk every morning to the office from Hammersmith – I was healthier. It irritates me to think how hard I work for no earthly benefit to myself. My money pleases a lot of people I don't care two straws about, and who are only my friends in the hope of making something out of me. If I could eat a hundred-guinea dinner myself every night, and enjoy it four hundred times as much as I used to enjoy a five-shilling dinner, there would be some sense in it. Why do I do it?"

I had never heard him talk like this before. In his excitement he rose from the table, and commenced pacing the room.

"Why don't I invest my money in the two and a half per cents?" he continued. "At the very worst I should be safe for five thousand a year. What, in the name of common sense, does a man want with more? I am always saying to myself, I'll do it; why don't I?"

"Well, why not?" I echoed.

"That's what I want you to tell me," he returned. "You set up for understanding human nature, it's a mystery to me. In my place, you would do as I do; you know that. If somebody left you a hundred thousand pounds to-morrow, you would start a newspaper, or build a theatre – some damn-fool trick for getting rid of the money and giving yourself seventeen hours' anxiety a day; you know you would."

I hung my head in shame. I felt the justice of the accusation. It has always been my dream to run a newspaper and own a theatre.

"If we worked only for what we could spend," he went on, "the City might put up its shutters to-morrow morning. What I want to get at the bottom of is this instinct that drives us to work apparently for work's own sake. What is this strange thing that gets upon our back and spurs us?"

A servant entered at that moment with a cablegram from the manager of one of his Austrian mines, and he had to leave me for his study. But, walking home, I fell to pondering on his words. *Why* this endless work? Why each morning do we get up and wash and dress ourselves, to undress ourselves at night and go to bed again? Why do we work merely to earn money to buy food; and eat food so as to gain strength that we may work? Why do we live, merely in the end to say good-bye to one another? Why do we labour to bring children into the world that they may die and be buried?

Of what use our mad striving, our passionate desire? Will it matter to the ages whether, once upon a time, the Union Jack or the Tricolour floated over the battlements of Badajoz? Yet we poured our blood into its ditches to decide the question. Will it matter, in the days when the glacial period shall have come again, to clothe the earth with silence, whose foot first trod the Pole? Yet, generation after generation, we mile its roadway with our whitening bones. So very soon the worms come to us; does it matter whether we love or hate? Yet the hot blood rushes through our veins, we wear out heart and brain for shadowy hopes that ever fade as we press forward.

The flower struggles up from seed-pod, draws the sweet sap from the ground, folds its petals each night, and sleeps. Then love comes to it in a strange form, and it longs to mingle its pollen with the pollen of some other flower. So it puts forth its gay blossoms, and the wandering insect bears the message from seed-pod to seed-pod. And the seasons pass, bringing with them the sunshine and the rain, till the flower withers, never having known the real purpose for which it lived, thinking the garden was made for it, not it for the garden. The coral insect dreams in its small soul, which is possibly its small stomach, of home and food. So it works and strives deep down in the dark waters, never knowing of the continents it is fashioning.

But the question still remains: for what purpose is it all? Science explains it to us. By ages of strife and effort we improve the race; from ether, through the monkey, man is born. So, through the labour of the coming ages, he will free himself still further from the brute. Through sorrow and through struggle, by the sweat of brain and brow, he will lift himself towards the angels. He will come into his kingdom.

But why the building? Why the passing of the countless ages? Why should he not have been born the god he is to be, imbued at birth with all the capabilities his ancestors have died acquiring? Why the Pict and Hun that *I* may be? Why *I*, that a descendant of my own, to whom I shall seem a savage, shall come after me? Why, if the universe be ordered by a Creator to whom all things are possible, the protoplasmic cell? Why not the man that is to be? Shall all the generations be so much human waste that he may live? Am I but another layer of the soil preparing for him?

Or, if our future be in other spheres, then why the need of this planet? Are we labouring at some work too vast for us to perceive? Are our passions and desires mere whips and traces by the help of which we are driven? Any theory seems more hopeful than the thought that all our eager, fretful lives are but the turning of a useless prison crank. Looking back the little distance that our dim eyes can penetrate the past, what do we find? Civilizations, built up with infinite care, swept aside and lost. Beliefs for which men lived and died, proved to be mockeries. Greek Art crushed to the dust by Gothic bludgeons. Dreams of fraternity, drowned in blood by a Napoleon. What is left to us, but the hope that the work itself, not the result, is the real monument? Maybe, we are as children, asking, "Of what use are these lessons? What good will they ever be to us?" But there comes a day when the lad understands why he learnt grammar and geography, when even dates have a meaning for him. But this is not until he has left school, and gone out into the wider world. So, perhaps, when we are a little more grown up, we too may begin to understand the reason for our living.

ON THE CARE AND MANAGEMENT
OF WOMEN

I talked to a woman once on the subject of honeymoons.
I said, "Would you recommend a long honeymoon, or a
Saturday to Monday somewhere?" A silence fell upon
her. I gathered she was looking back rather than forward
to her answer.

"I would advise a long honeymoon," she replied at
length, "the old-fashioned month."

"Why," I persisted, "I thought the tendency of the age
was to cut these things shorter and shorter."

"It is the tendency of the age," she answered, "to seek
escape from many things it would be wiser to face. I
think myself that, for good or evil, the sooner it is over –
the sooner both the man and the woman know – the
better."

"The sooner what is over?" I asked.

If she had a fault, this woman, about which I am not
sure, it was an inclination towards enigma.

She crossed to the window and stood there, looking
out.

"Was there not a custom," she said, still gazing down
into the wet, glistening street, "among one of the ancient
peoples, I forget which, ordaining that when a man and
woman, loving one another, or thinking that they loved,
had been joined together, they should go down upon
their wedding night to the temple? And into the dark

recesses of the temple, through many winding passages, the priest led them until they came to the great chamber where dwelt the voice of their god. There the priest left them, clanging-to the massive door behind him, and there, alone in silence, they made their sacrifice; and in the night the Voice spoke to them, showing them their future life – whether they had chosen well; whether their love would live or die. And in the morning the priest returned and led them back into the day; and they dwelt among their fellows. But no one was permitted to question them, nor they to answer should any do so. Well, do you know, our nineteenth-century honeymoon at Brighton, Switzerland, or Ramsgate, as the choice or necessity may be, always seems to me merely another form of that night spent alone in the temple before the altar of that forgotten god. Our young men and women marry, and we kiss them and congratulate them; and, standing on the doorstep, throw rice and old slippers, and shout good wishes after them; and he waves his gloved hand to us, and she flutters her little handkerchief from the carriage window; and we watch their smiling faces and hear their laughter until the corner hides them from our view. Then we go about our own business, and a short time passes by; and one day we meet them again, and their faces have grown older and graver; and I always wonder what the Voice has told them during that little while that they have been absent from our sight. But of course it would not do to ask them. Nor would they answer truly if we did."

My friend laughed, and, leaving the window, took her place beside the tea-things, and other callers dropping in, we fell to talk of pictures, plays, and people.

But I felt it would be unwise to act on her sole advice, much as I have always valued her opinion.

A woman takes life too seriously. It is a serious affair to most of us, the Lord knows. That is why it is well not to take it more seriously than need be.

Little Jack and little Jill fall down the hill, hurting their little knees, and their little noses, spilling the hard-earned water. We are very philosophical.

"Oh, don't cry!" we tell them, "that is babyish. Little boys and little girls must learn to bear pain. Up you get, fill the pail again, and try once more."

Little Jack and little Jill rub their dirty knuckles into their little eyes, looking ruefully at their bloody little knees, and trot back with the pail. We laugh at them, but not ill-naturedly.

"Poor little souls," we say; "how they did hullabaloo. One might have thought they were half-killed. And it was only a broken crown, after all. What a fuss children make!" We bear with much stoicism the fall of little Jack and little Jill.

But when *we* – grown-up Jack with moustache turning grey; grown-up Jill with the first faint "crows feet" showing – when *we* tumble down the hill, and *our* pail is spilt. Ye Heavens! what a tragedy has happened. Put out the stars, turn off the sun, suspend the laws of nature. Mr. Jack and Mrs. Jill, coming down the hill – what they were doing on the hill we will not inquire – have slipped over a stone, placed there surely by the evil powers of the universe. Mr. Jack and Mrs. Jill have bumped their silly heads. Mr. Jack and Mrs. Jill have hurt their little hearts, and stand marvelling that the world can go about its business in the face of such disaster.

Don't take the matter quite so seriously, Jack and Jill. You have spilled your happiness, you must toil up the hill again and refill the pail. Carry it more carefully next time. What were you doing? Playing some fool's trick, I'll be bound.

A laugh and a sigh, a kiss and good-bye, is our life. Is it worth so much fretting? It is a merry life on the whole. Courage, comrade. A campaign cannot be all drum and fife and stirrup-cup. The marching and the fighting must come into it somewhere. There are pleasant bivouacs among the vineyards, merry nights around the camp fires. White hands wave a welcome to us; bright eyes dim at our going. Would you run from the battle-music? What have you to complain of? Forward: the medal to some, the surgeon's knife to others; to all of us, sooner or later, six feet of mother earth. What are you afraid of? Courage, comrade.

There is a mean between basking through life with the smiling contentment of the alligator, and shivering through it with the aggressive sensibility of the Lama determined to die at every cross word. To bear it as a man we must also feel it as a man. My philosophic friend, seek not to comfort a brother standing by the coffin of his child with the cheery suggestion that it will be all the same a hundred years hence, because, for one thing, the observation is not true: the man is changed for all eternity – possibly for the better, but don't add that. A soldier with a bullet in his neck is never quite the man he was. But he can laugh and he can talk, drink his wine and ride his horse. Now and again, towards evening, when the weather is trying, the sickness will come upon him. You will find him on a couch in a dark corner.

"Hallo! old fellow, anything up?"

"Oh, just a twinge, the old wound, you know. I will be better in a little while."

Shut the door of the dark room quietly. I should not stay even to sympathize with him if I were you. The men will be coming to screw the coffin down soon. I think he would like to be alone with it till then. Let us leave him. He will come back to the club later on in the season. For a while we may have to give him another ten points or so, but he will soon get back his old form. Now and again, when he meets the other fellows' boys shouting on the towing-path; when Brown rushes up the drive, paper in hand, to tell him how that young scapegrace Jim has won his Cross; when he is congratulating Jones's eldest on having passed with honours, the old wound may give him a nasty twinge.

But the pain will pass away. He will laugh at our stories and tell us his own; eat his dinner, play his rubber. It is only a wound.

Tommy can never be ours, Jenny does not love us. We cannot afford claret, so we will have to drink beer. Well, what would you have us do? Yes, let us curse Fate by all means – some one to curse is always useful. Let us cry and wring our hands – for how long? The dinner-bell will ring soon, and the Smiths are coming. We shall have to talk about the opera and the picture-galleries. Quick, where is the eau-de-Cologne? where are the curling-tongs? Or would you we committed suicide? Is it worth while? Only a few more years – perhaps to-morrow, by aid of a piece of orange peel or a broken chimney-pot – and Fate will save us all that trouble.

Or shall we, as sulky children, mope day after day? We are a broken-hearted little Jack – little Jill. We will never smile again; we will pine away and die, and be buried in the spring. The world is sad, and life so cruel, and heaven so cold. Oh dear! oh dear! we have hurt ourselves.

We whimper and whine at every pain. In old strong days men faced real dangers, real troubles every hour; they had no time to cry. Death and disaster stood ever at the door. Men were contemptuous of them. Now in each snug protected villa we set to work to make wounds out of scratches. Every headache becomes an agony, every heartache a tragedy. It took a murdered father, a drowned sweetheart, a dishonoured mother, a ghost, and a slaughtered Prime Mnister to produce the emotions in Hamlet that a modern minor poet obtains from a chorus girl's frown, or a temporary slump on the Stock Exchange. Like Mrs. Gummidge, we feel it more. The lighter and easier life gets the more seriously we go out to meet it. The boatmen of Ulysses faced the thunder and the sunshine alike with frolic welcome. We modern sailors have grown more sensitive. The sunshine scorches us, the rain chills us. We meet both with loud self-pity.

Thinking these thoughts, I sought a second friend – a man whose breezy common-sense has often helped me, and him likewise I questioned on this subject of honeymoons.

"My dear boy," he replied; "take my advice, if ever you get married, arrange it so that the honeymoon shall only last a week, and let it be a bustling week into the bargain. Take a Cook's circular tour. Get married on the Saturday morning, cut the breakfast and all that foolishness, and catch the eleven-ten from Charing Cross to Paris. Take her up the Eiffel Tower on Sunday. Lunch at Fontainebleau. Dine at the Maison Dorée, and show her the Moulin Rouge in the evening. Take the night train for Lucerne. Devote Monday and Tuesday to doing Switzerland, and get into Rome by Thursday morning, taking the Italian lakes *en route*. On Friday cross to Marseilles, and from there push along to Monte Carlo. Let her have a flutter at the tables. Start early Saturday morning for Spain, cross the Pyrenees on mules, and rest at Bordeaux on Sunday. Get back to Paris on Monday (Monday is always a good day for the opera), and on Tuesday evening you will be at home, and glad to get there. Don't give her time to criticize you until she has got used to you. No man will bear unprotected exposure to a young girl's eyes. The honeymoon is the matrimonial microscope. Wobble it. Confuse it with many objects. Cloud it with other interests. Don't sit still to be examined. Besides, remember that a man always appears at his best when active, and a woman at her worst. Bustle her, my dear boy, bustle her: I don't care who she may be. Give her plenty of luggage to look after; make her catch trains. Let her see the average husband sprawling comfortably over the railway cushions, while his wife has to sit bolt upright in the corner left to her. Let her hear how other men swear. Let her smell other men's tobacco. Hurry up, and get her accustomed quickly to the sight of mankind. Then she will be less surprised and shocked as she grows to know you. One of the best fellows I ever knew spoilt his married life beyond repair by a long quiet honeymoon. They went off for a month to a lonely cottage in some heaven-forsaken spot, where never a soul came near them, and never a thing happened but morning, afternoon, and night. There for thirty days she overhauled him. When he yawned – and he yawned pretty often, I guess, during that month – she thought of the size of his mouth, and when he put his heels upon the fender she sat and brooded upon the shape of his feet. At meal-time, not feeling hungry herself, having nothing to do to make her hungry, she would occupy herself with watching him eat; and at night, not feeling sleepy for the same reason, she would lie awake and listen to his snoring. After the first day or two he grew tired of talking nonsense, and she of listening to it (it sounded nonsense now they could speak it aloud; they had fancied it poetry when they had had to whisper it); and having no other subject, as yet, of common interest, they would sit and stare in front of them in silence. One day some trifle irritated him and he swore. On a busy railway platform, or in a crowded hotel, she would have said, 'Oh!' and they would both have laughed. From that echoing desert the silly words rose up in widening circles towards the sky, and that night she cried herself to sleep. Bustle them, my dear boy, bustle them. We all like each other better the less we think about one another, and the honeymoon is an exceptionally critical time. Bustle her, my dear boy, bustle her."

My very worst honeymoon experience took place in the South of England in eighteen hundred and – well, never mind the exact date, let us say a few years ago. I was a shy young man at that time. Many complain of my reserve to this day, but then some girls expect too much from a man. We all have our shortcomings. Even then, however, I was not so shy as she. We had to travel from Lyndhurst in the New Forest to Ventnor, an awkward bit of cross-country work in those days.

"It's so fortunate you are going too," said her aunt to me on the Tuesday; "Minnie is always nervous travelling alone. You will be able to look after her, and I shan't be anxious."

I said it would be a pleasure, and at the time I honestly thought it. On the Wednesday I went down to the coach office, and booked two places for Lymington, from where we took the steamer. I had not a suspicion of trouble.

The booking-clerk was an elderly man. He said –

"I've got the box seat, and the end place on the back bench."

I said – "Oh, can't I have two together."

He was a kindly-looking old fellow. He winked at me. I wondered all the way home why he had winked at me. He said –

"I'll manage it somehow."

I said – "It's very kind of you, I'm sure."

He laid his hand on my shoulder. He struck me as familiar, but well-intentioned. He said –

"We have all of us been there."

I thought he was alluding to the Isle of Wight. I said –

"And this is the best time of the year for it, so I'm told." It was early summer time.

He said – "It's all right in summer, and it's good enough in winter – *while it lasts*. You make the most of it, young 'un;" and he slapped me on the back and laughed.

He would have irritated me in another minute. I paid for the seats and left him.

At half-past eight the next morning Minnie and I started for the coach-office. I call her Minnie, not with any wish to be impertinent, but because I have forgotten her surname. It must be ten years since I last saw her. She was a pretty girl, too, with those brown eyes that always cloud before they laugh. Her aunt did not drive down with us as she had intended, in consequence of a headache. She was good enough to say she felt every confidence in me.

The old booking-clerk caught sight of us when we were about a quarter of a mile away, and drew to us the attention of the coachman, who communicated the fact of our approach to the gathered passengers. Everybody left off talking, and waited for us. The boots seized his horn, and blew – one could hardly call it a blast; it would be difficult to say what he blew. He put his heart into it, but not sufficient wind. I think his intention was to welcome us, but it suggested rather a feeble curse. We learnt subsequently that he was a beginner on the instrument.

In some mysterious way the whole affair appeared to be our party. The booking-clerk bustled up and helped Minnie from the cart. I feared, for a moment, he was going to kiss her. The coachman grinned when I said good-morning to him. The passengers grinned, the boots grinned. Two chamber-maids and a waiter came out from the hotel, and they grinned. I drew Minnie aside, and whispered to her. I said –

"There's something funny about us. All these people are grinning."

She walked round me, and I walked round her, but we could neither of us discover anything amusing about the other. The booking clerk said –

"It's all right. I've got you young people two places just behind the box-seat. We'll have to put five of you on that seat. You won't mind sitting a bit close, will you?"

The booking-clerk winked at the coachman, the coachman winked at the passengers, the passengers winked at one another – those of them who could wink – and everybody laughed. The two chamber-maids became hysterical, and had to cling to each other for support. With the exception of Minnie and myself, it seemed to be the merriest coach party ever assembled at Lyndhurst.

We had taken our places, and I was still busy trying to fathom the joke, when a stout lady appeared on the scene, and demanded to know her place.

The clerk explained to her that it was in the middle behind the driver.

"We've had to put five of you on that seat," added the clerk.

The stout lady looked at the seat.

"Five of us can't squeeze into that," she said.

Five of her certainly could not. Four ordinary sized people with her would find it tight.

"Very well then," said the clerk, "you can have the end place on the back seat."

"Nothing of the sort," said the stout lady. "I booked my seat on Monday, and you told me any of the front places were vacant."

"*I'll* take the back place," I said, "I don't mind it."

"You stop where you are, young 'un," said the clerk, firmly, "and don't be a fool. I'll fix *her*."

I objected to his language, but his tone was kindness itself.

"Oh, let *me* have the back seat," said Minnie, rising, "I'd so like it."

For answer the coachman put both his hands on her shoulders. He was a heavy man, and she sat down again.

"Now then, mum," said the clerk, addressing the stout lady, "are you going up there in the middle, or are you coming up here at the back?"

"But why not let one of them take the back seat?" demanded the stout lady, pointing her recticule at Minnie and myself; "they say they'd like it. Let them have it."

The coachman rose, and addressed his remarks generally.

"Put her up at the back, or leave her behind," he directed. "Man and wife have never been separated on this coach since I started running it fifteen year ago, and they ain't going to be now."

A general cheer greeted this sentiment. The stout lady, now regarded as a would-be blighter of love's young dream, was hustled into the back seat, the whip cracked, and away we rolled.

So here was the explanation. We were in a honeymoon district, in June – the most popular month in the whole year for marriage. Every two out of three couples found wandering about the New Forest in June are honeymoon couples; the third are going to be. When they travel anywhere it is to the Isle of Wight. We both had on new clothes. Our bags happened to be new. By some evil chance our very umbrellas were new. Our united ages were thirty-seven. The wonder would have been had we *not* been mistaken for a young married couple.

A day of greater misery I have rarely passed. To Minnie, so her aunt informed me afterwards, the journey was the most terrible experience of her life, but then her experience, up to that time, had been limited. She was engaged, and devotedly attached, to a young clergyman; I was madly in love with a somewhat plump girl named Cecilia, who lived with her mother at Hampstead. I am positive as to her living at Hampstead. I remember so distinctly my weekly walk down the hill from Church Row to the Swiss Cottage station. When walking down a steep hill all the weight of the body is forced into the toe of the boot, and when the boot is two sizes too small for you, and you have been living in it since the early afternoon, you remember a thing like that. But all my recollections of Cecilia are painful, and it is needless to pursue them.

Our coach-load was a homely party, and some of the jokes were broad – harmless enough in themselves, had Minnie and I really been the married couple we were supposed to be, but even in that case unnecessary. I can only hope that Minnie did not understand them. Anyhow, she looked as if she didn't.

I forget where we stopped for lunch, but I remember that lamb and mint sauce was on the table, and that the circumstance afforded the greatest delight to all the party, with the exception of the stout lady, who was still indignant, Minnie and myself. About my behaviour as a bridegroom opinion appeared to be divided. "He's a bit stand-offish with her," I overheard one lady remark to her husband; "I like to see 'em a bit kittenish myself." A young waitress, on the other hand, I am happy to say, showed more sense of natural reserve. "Well, I respect him for it," she was saying to the barmaid, as we passed through the hall; "I'd just hate to be fuzzled over with everybody looking on." Nobody took the trouble to drop their voices for our benefit. We might have been a pair of prize love birds on exhibition, the way we were openly discussed. By the majority we were clearly regarded as a sulky young couple who would not go through their tricks.

I have often wondered since how a real married couple would have faced the situation. Possibly, had we consented to give a short display of marital affection, "by desire," we might have been left in peace for the remainder of the journey.

Our reputation preceded us on to the steamboat. Minnie begged and prayed me to let it be known we were not married. How I was to let it be known, except by requesting the captain to summon the whole ship's company on deck, and then making them a short speech, I could not think. Minnie said she could not bear it any longer, and retired to the ladies' cabin. She went off crying. Her trouble was attributed by crew and passengers to my coldness. One fool planted himself opposite me with his legs apart, and shook his head at me.

"Go down and comfort her," he began. "Take an old man's advice. Put your arms around her." (He was one of those sentimental idiots.) "Tell her that you love her."

I told him to go and hang himself, with so much vigour that he all but fell overboard. He was saved by a poultry crate: I had no luck that day.

At Ryde the guard, by superhuman effort, contrived to keep us a carriage to ourselves. I gave him a shilling, because I did not know what else to do. I would have made it half-a-sovereign if he had put eight other passengers in with us. At every station people came to the window to look in at us.

I handed Minnie over to her father on Ventnor platform; and I took the first train, the next morning, to London. I felt I did not want to see her again for a little while; and I felt convinced she could do without a visit from me. Our next meeting took place the week before her marriage.

"Where are you going to spend your honeymoon?" I asked her; "in the New Forest?"

"No," she replied; "nor in the Isle of Wight."

To enjoy the humour of an incident one must be at some distance from it either in time or relationship. I remember watching an amusing scene in Whitefield Street, just off Tottenham Court Road, one winter's Saturday night. A woman – a rather respectable looking woman, had her hat only been on straight – had just been shot out of a public-house. She was very dignified, and very drunk. A policeman requested her to move on. She called him "Fellow," and demanded to know of him if he considered that was the proper tone in which to address a lady. She threatened to report him to her cousin, the Lord Chancellor.

"Yes; this way to the Lord Chancellor," retorted the policeman "You come along with me;" and he caught hold of her by the arm.

She gave a lurch, and nearly fell. To save her the man put his arm round her waist. She clasped him round the neck, and together they spun round two or three times; while at the very moment a piano-organ at the opposite corner struck up a waltz.

"Choose your partners, gentlemen, for the next dance," shouted a wag, and the crowd roared.

I was laughing myself, for the situation was undeniably comical, the constable's expression of disgust being quite Hogarthian, when the sight of a child's face beneath the gas-lamp stayed me. Her look was so full of terror that I tried to comfort her.

"It's only a drunken woman," I said; "he's not going to hurt her."

"Please, sir," was the answer, "it's my mother."

Our joke is generally another's pain. The man who sits down on the tin-tack rarely joins in the laugh.

ON THE MINDING OF OTHER
PEOPLE'S BUSINESS

I walked one bright September morning in the Strand. I love London best in the autumn. Then only can one see the gleam of its white pavements, the bold, unbroken outline of its streets. I love the cool vistas one comes across of mornings in the parks, the soft twilights that linger in the empty bye streets. In June the restaurant manager is off-hand with me; I feel I am but in his way. In August he spreads for me the table by the window, pours out for me my wine with his own fat hands. I cannot doubt his regard for me: my foolish jealousies are stilled. Do I care for a drive after dinner through the caressing night air, I can climb the omnibus stair without a preliminary fight upon the curb, can sit with easy conscience and unsquashed body, not feeling I have deprived some hot, tired woman of a seat. Do I desire the play, no harsh, forbidding "House full" board repels me from the door. During her season, London, a harassed hostess, has no time for us, her intimates. Her rooms are overcrowded, her servants overworked, her dinners hurriedly cooked, her tone insincere. In the spring, to be truthful, the great lady condescends to be somewhat vulgar – noisy and ostentatious. Not till the guests are departed is she herself again, the London that we, her children, love.

Have you, gentle Reader, ever seen London – not the London of the waking day, coated with crawling life, as a blossom with blight, but the London of the morning, freed from her rags, the patient city, clad in mists? Get you up with the dawn one Sunday in summer time. Wake none else, but creep down stealthily into the kitchen, and make your own tea and toast.

Be careful you stumble not over the cat. She will worm herself insidiously between your legs. It is her way; she means it in friendship. Neither bark your shins against the coal-box. Why the kitchen coal-box has its fixed place in the direct line between the kitchen door and the gas-bracket I cannot say. I merely know it as an universal law; and I would that you escaped that coal-box, lest the frame of mind I desire for you on this Sabbath morning be dissipated.

A spoon to stir your tea, I fear you must dispense with. Knives and forks you will discover in plenty; blacking brushes you will put your hand upon in every drawer; of emery paper, did one require it, there are reams; but it is a point with every house-keeper that the spoons be hidden in a different place each night. If anybody excepting herself can find them in the morning, it is a slur upon her. No matter, a stick of firewood, sharpened at one end, makes an excellent substitute.

Your breakfast done, turn out the gas, remount the stairs quietly, open gently the front door and slip out. You will find yourself in an unknown land. A strange city has grown round you in the night.

The sweet long streets lie silent in the sunlight. Not a living thing is to be seen save some lean Tom that slinks from his gutter feast as you approach. From some tree there will sound perhaps a fretful chirp: but the London sparrow is no early riser; he is but talking in his sleep. The slow tramp of an unseen policeman draws near or dies away. The clatter of your own footsteps goes with you, troubling you. You find yourself trying to walk softly, as one does in echoing cathedrals. A voice is everywhere about you whispering to you "Hush." Is this million-breasted City then some tender Artemis, seeking to keep her babes asleep? "Hush, you careless wayfarer; do not waken them. Walk lighter; they are so tired, these myriad children of mine, sleeping in my thousand arms. They are over-worked and over-worried; so many of them are sick, so many fretful, many of them, alas, so full of naughtiness. But all of them so tired. Hush! they worry me with their noise and riot when they are awake. They are so good now they are asleep. Walk lightly, let them rest."

Where the ebbing tide flows softly through worn arches to the sea, you may hear the stone-faced City talking to the restless waters: "Why will you never stay with me? Why come but to go?"

"I cannot say, I do not understand. From the deep sea I come, but only as a bird loosed from a child's hand with a cord. When she calls I must return."

"It is so with these children of mine. They come to me, I know not whence. I nurse them for a little while, till a hand I do not see plucks them back. And others take their place."

Through the still air there passes a ripple of sound. The sleeping City stirs with a faint sigh. A distant milk-cart rattling by raises a thousand echoes; it is the vanguard of a yoked army. Soon from every street there rises the soothing cry, "Mee'hilk – mee'hilk." London, like some Gargantuan babe, is awake, crying for its milk. These be the white-smocked nurses hastening with its morning nourishment. The early church bells ring. "You have had your milk, little London. Now come and say your prayers. Another week has just begun, baby London. God knows what will happen, say your prayers."

One by one the little creatures creep from behind the blinds into the streets. The brooding tenderness is vanished from the City's face. The fretful noises of the day have come again. Silence, her lover of the night, kisses her stone lips, and steals away. And you, gentle Reader, return home, garlanded with the self-sufficiency of the early riser.

But it was of a certain week-day morning in the Strand
that I was thinking. I was standing outside Gatti's
Restaurant, where I had just breakfasted, listening
leisurely to an argument between an indignant lady
passenger, presumably of Irish extraction, and an
omnibus conductor.

"For what d'ye want thin to paint Putney on ye'r bus, if
ye don't *go* to Putney?" said the lady.

"We *do* go to Putney," said the conductor.

"Thin why did ye put me out here?"

"I didn't put you out, yer got out."

"Shure, didn't the gintleman in the corner tell me I
was comin' further away from Putney ivery minit?"

"Wal, and so yer was."

"Thin whoy didn't you tell me?"

"How was I to know yer wanted to go to Putney? Yer
sings out Putney, and I stops and in yer dumps."

"And for what d'ye think I called out Putney thin?"

"'Cause it's my name, or rayther the bus's name? This
'ere *is* a Putney."

"How can it be a Putney whin it isn't goin' to Putney,
ye gomerhawk?"

"Ain't you an Hirishwoman?" retorted the conductor.

"'Course yer are. But yer aren't always goin' to Ireland.
We're goin' to Putney in time, only we're a-going to
Liverpool Street fust. 'Igher up, Jim."

The bus moved on, and I was about to cross the road,
when a man, muttering savagely to himself, walked into
me. He would have swept past me had I not, recognizing
him, arrested him. It was my friend B——, a busy editor
of magazines and journals. It was some seconds before he
appeared able to struggle out of his abstraction, and
remember himself. "Halloo," he then said, "who would
have thought of seeing *you* here?"

"To judge by the way you were walking," I replied,
"one would imagine the Strand the last place in which
you expected to see any human being. Do you ever walk
into a short-tempered, muscular man?"

"Did I walk into you?" he asked surprised.

"Well, not right in," I answered, "if we are to be literal. You walked on to me; if I had not stopped you, I suppose you would have walked over me."

"It is this confounded Christmas business," he explained. "It drives me off my head."

"I have heard Christmas advanced as an excuse for many things," I replied, "but not early in September."

"Oh, you know what I mean," he answered, "we are in the middle of our Christmas number. I am working day and night upon it. By the bye," he added, "that puts me in mind. I am arranging a symposium, and I want you to join. 'Should Christmas,'" – I interrupted him.

"My dear fellow," I said, "I commenced my journalistic career when I was eighteen, and I have continued it at intervals ever since. I have written about Christmas from the sentimental point of view; I have analyzed it from the philosophical point of view; and I have scarified it from the sarcastic standpoint. I have treated Christmas humorously for the Comics, and sympathetically for the Provincial Weeklies. I have said all that is worth saying on the subject of Christmas – maybe a trifle more. I have told the new-fashioned Christmas story – you know the sort of thing: your heroine tries to understand herself, and, failing, runs off with the man who began as the hero; your good woman turns out to be really bad when one comes to know her; while the villain, the only decent person in the story, dies with an enigmatic sentence on his lips that looks as if it meant something, but which you yourself would be sorry to have to explain. I have also written the old-fashioned Christmas story – you know that also; you begin with a good old-fashioned snowstorm; you have a good old-fashioned squire, and he lives in a good old-fashioned Hall; you work in a good old-fashioned murder; and end up with a good old-fashioned Christmas dinner. I have gathered Christmas guests together round the crackling logs to tell ghost stories to each other on Christmas Eve, while without the wind howled, as it always does on these occasions, at its proper cue. I have sent children to Heaven on Christmas Eve – it must be quite a busy time for St. Peter, Christmas morning, so many good children die on Christmas Eve. It has always been a popular night with them. – I have revivified dead lovers and brought them back well and jolly, just in time to sit down to the Christmas dinner. I am not ashamed of having done these things. At the time I thought them good. I once loved currant wine and girls with tousley hair. One's views change as one grows older. I have discussed Christmas as a religious festival. I have arranged it as a social incubus. If there be any joke connected with Christmas that I have not already made I should be glad to hear it. I have trotted out the indigestion jokes till the sight of one of them gives me indigestion myself. I have ridiculed the family gathering. I have scoffed at the Christmas present. I have made witty use of paterfamilias and his bills. I have —"

"Did I ever show you," I broke off to ask as we were crossing the Haymarket, "that little parody of mine on Poe's poem of 'The Bells'? It begins –" He interrupted me in his turn –

"Bills, bills, bills," he repeated.

"You are quite right," I admitted. "I forgot I ever showed it to you."

"You never did," he replied.

"Then how do you know how it begins?" I asked.

"I don't know for certain," he admitted, "but I get, on an average, sixty-five a year submitted to me, and they all begin that way. I thought, perhaps, yours did also."

"I don't see how else it could begin," I retorted. He had rather annoyed me. "Besides, it doesn't matter how a poem begins. It is how it goes on that is the important thing; and anyhow, I'm not going to write you anything about Christmas. Ask me to make you a new joke about a plumber; suggest my inventing something original and not too shocking for a child to say about heaven; propose my running you off a dog story that can be believed by a man of average determination, and we may come to terms. But on the subject of Christmas I am taking a rest."

By this time we had reached Piccadilly Circus.

"I don't blame you," he said, "if you are as sick of the subject as I am. So soon as these Christmas numbers are off my mind, and Christmas is over till next June at the office, I shall begin it at home. The housekeeping is gone up a pound a week already. I know what that means. The dear little woman is saving up to give me an expensive present that I don't want. I think the presents are the worst part of Christmas. Emma will give me a water-colour that she has painted herself. She always does. There would be no harm in that if she did not expect me to hang it in the drawing room. Have you ever seen my cousin Emma's water-colours?" he asked.

"I think I have," I replied.

"There's no thinking about it," he retorted angrily. "They're not the sort of water-colours you forget."

He apostrophized the Circus generally.

"Why do people do these things?" he demanded. "Even an amateur artist must have *some* sense. Can't they see what is happening? There's that thing of hers hanging in the passage. I put it in the passage because there's not much light in the passage. She's labelled it Reverie. If she had called it Influenza I could have understood it. I asked her where she got the idea from, and she said she saw the sky like that one evening in Norfolk. Great Heavens! then why didn't she shut her eyes, or go home and hide behind the bed-curtains? If I had seen a sky like that in Norfolk I should have taken the first train back to London. I suppose the poor girl can't help seeing these things, but why paint them?"

I said, "I suppose painting is a necessity to some natures."

"But why give the things to me?" he pleaded.

I could offer him no adequate reason.

"The idiotic presents that people give you!" he continued. "I said I'd like Tennyson's poems one year. They had worried me to know what I did want. I didn't want anything really; that was the only thing I could think of that I wasn't dead sure I didn't want. Well, they clubbed together, four of them, and gave me Tennyson in twelve volumes, illustrated with coloured photographs. They meant kindly, of course. If you suggest a tobacco-pouch they give you a blue velvet bag capable of holding about a pound, embroidered with flowers, life-size. The only way one could use it would be to put a strap to it and wear it as a satchel. Would you believe it, I have got a velvet smoking-jacket, ornamented with forget-me-nots and butterflies in coloured silk; I'm not joking. And they ask me why I never wear it. I'll bring it down to the Club one of these nights and wake the place up a bit: it needs it."

We had arrived by this at the steps of the 'Devonshire.'

"And I'm just as bad," he went on, "when I give presents. I never give them what they want. I never hit upon anything that is of any use to anybody. If I give Jane a chinchilla tippet, you may be certain chinchilla is the most out-of-date fur that any woman could wear. 'Oh! that is nice of you,' she says; 'now that is just the very thing I wanted. I will keep it by me till chinchilla comes in again.' I give the girls watch-chains when nobody is wearing watch-chains. When watch-chains are all the rage I give them ear-rings, and they thank me, and suggest my taking them to a fancy-dress ball, that being their only chance to wear the confounded things. I waste money on white gloves with black backs, to find that white gloves with black backs stamp a woman as suburban. I believe all the shop-keepers in London save their old stock to palm it off on me at Christmas time. And why does it always take half-a-dozen people to serve you with a pair of gloves, I'd like to know? Only last week Jane asked me to get her some gloves for that last Mansion House affair. I was feeling amiable, and I thought I would do the thing handsomely. I hate going into a draper's shop; everybody stares at a man as if he were forcing his way into the ladies' department of a Turkish bath. One of those marionette sort of men came up to me and said it was a fine morning. What the devil did I want to talk about the morning to him for? I said I wanted some gloves. I described them to the best of my recollection. I said, 'I want them four buttons, but they are not to be button-gloves; the buttons are in the middle and they reach up to the elbow, if you know what I mean.' He bowed, and said he understood exactly what I meant, which was a damned sight more than I did. I told him I wanted three pair cream and three pair fawn-coloured, and the fawn-coloured were to be swedes. He corrected me. He said I meant 'Suede.' I dare say he was right, but the interruption put me off, and I had to begin over again. He listened attentively until I had finished. I guess I was about five minutes standing with him there close to the door. He said, 'Is that all you require, sir, this morning?' I said it was.

"'Thank you, sir,' he replied. 'This way, please, sir.'

"He took me into another room, and there we met a man named Jansen, to whom he briefly introduced me as a gentleman who 'desired gloves.' 'Yes, sir,' said Mr. Jansen; 'and what sort of gloves do you desire?'

"I told him I wanted six pairs altogether – three suede, fawn-coloured, and three cream-coloured – kids.

"He said, 'Do you mean kid gloves, sir, or gloves for children?'

"He made me angry by that. I told him I was not in the habit of using slang. Nor am I when buying gloves. He said he was sorry. I explained to him about the buttons, so far as I could understand it myself, and about the length. I asked him to see to it that the buttons were sewn on firmly, and that the stitching everywhere was perfect, adding that the last gloves my wife had had of his firm had been most unsatisfactory. Jane had impressed upon me to add that. She said it would make them more careful.

"He listened to me in rapt ecstasy. I might have been music.

"'And what size, sir?' he asked.

"I had forgotten that. 'Oh, sixes,' I answered, 'unless they are very stretchy indeed, in which case they had better be five and three-quarter.'

"'Oh, and the stitching on the cream is to be black,' I added. That was another thing I had forgotten.

"'Thank you very much,' said Mr. Jansen; 'is there anything else that you require this morning?'

"'No, thank you,' I replied, 'not this morning.' I was beginning to like the man.

"He took me for quite a walk, and wherever we went everybody left off what they were doing to stare at me. I was getting tired when we reached the glove department. He marched me up to a young man who was sticking pins into himself. He said 'Gloves,' and disappeared through a curtain. The young man left off sticking pins into himself, and leant across the counter.

"'Ladies' gloves or gentlemen's gloves?' he said.

"Well, I was pretty mad by this time, as you can guess. It is funny when you come to think of it afterwards, but the wonder then was that I didn't punch his head.

"I said, 'Are you ever busy in this shop? Does there ever come a time when you feel you would like to get your work done, instead of lingering over it and spinning it out for pure love of the thing?'

"He did not appear to understand me. I said, 'I met a man at your door a quarter of an hour ago, and we talked about these gloves that I want, and I told him all my ideas on the subject. He took me to your Mr. Jansen, and Mr. Jansen and I went over the whole business again. Now Mr. Jansen leaves me with you – *you* who do not even know whether I want ladies' or gentlemen's gloves. Before I go over this story for the third time, I want to know whether you are the man who is going to serve me, or whether you are merely a listener, because personally I am tired of the subject?'

"Well, this was the right man at last, and I got my gloves from him. But what is the explanation – what is the idea? I was in that shop from first to last five-and-thirty minutes. And then a fool took me out the wrong way to show me a special line in sleeping-socks. I told him I was not requiring any. He said he didn't want me to buy, he only wanted me to see them. No wonder the drapers have had to start luncheon and tea-rooms. They'll fix up small furnished flats soon, where a woman can live for a week."

I said it was very trying, shopping. I also said, as he invited me, and as he appeared determined to go on talking, that I would have a brandy-and-soda. We were in the smoke-room by this time.

"There ought to be an association," he continued, "a kind of clearing-house for the collection and distribution of Christmas presents. One would give them a list of the people from whom to collect presents, and of the people to whom to send. Suppose they collected on my account twenty Christmas presents, value, say, ten pounds, while on the other hand they sent out for me thirty presents at a cost of fifteen pounds. They would debit me with the balance of five pounds, together with a small commission. I should pay it cheerfully, and there would be no further trouble. Perhaps one might even make a profit. The idea might include birthdays and weddings. A firm would do the business thoroughly. They would see that all your friends paid up – I mean sent presents; and they would not forget to send to your most important relative. There is only one member of our family capable of leaving a shilling; and of course if I forget to send to any one it is to him. When I remember him I generally make a muddle of the business. Two years ago I gave him a bath – I don't mean I washed him – an india-rubber thing, that he could pack in his portmanteau. I thought he would find it useful for travelling. Would you believe it, he took it as a personal affront, and wouldn't speak to me for a month, the snuffy old idiot."

"I suppose the children enjoy it," I said.

"Enjoy what?" he asked.

"Why, Christmas," I explained.

"I don't believe they do," he snapped; "nobody enjoys it. We excite them for three weeks beforehand, telling them what a good time they are going to have, over-feed them for two or three days, take them to something they do not want to see, but which we do, and then bully them for a fortnight to get them back into their normal condition. I was always taken to the Crystal Palace and Madame Tussaud's when I was a child, I remember. How I did hate that Crystal Palace! Aunt used to superintend. It was always a bitterly cold day, and we always got into the wrong train, and travelled half the day before we got there. We never had any dinner. It never occurs to a woman that anybody can want their meals while away from home. She seems to think that nature is in suspense from the time you leave the house till the time you get back to it. A bun and a glass of milk was her idea of lunch for a school-boy. Half her time was taken up in losing us, and the other half in slapping us when she had found us. The only thing we really enjoyed was the row with the cabman coming home."

I rose to go.

"Then you won't join that symposium?" said B——. "It would be an easy enough thing to knock off – 'Why Christmas should be abolished.'"

"It sounds simple," I answered. "But how do you propose to abolish it?" The lady editor of an "advanced" American magazine once set the discussion – "Should sex be abolished?" and eleven ladies and gentlemen seriously argued the question.

"Leave it to die of inanition," said B——; "the first step is to arouse public opinion. Convince the public that it should be abolished."

"But why should it be abolished?" I asked.

"Great Scott! man," he exclaimed; "don't you want it abolished?"

"I'm not sure that I do," I replied.

"Not sure," he retorted; "you call yourself a journalist, and admit there is a subject under Heaven of which you are not sure!"

"It has come over me of late years," I replied. "It used not to be my failing, as you know."

He glanced round to make sure we were out of earshot, then sunk his voice to a whisper.

"Between ourselves," he said, "I'm not so sure of everything myself as I used to be. Why is it?"

"Perhaps we are getting older," I suggested.

He said – "I started golf last year, and the first time I took the club in my hand I sent the ball a furlong. 'It seems an easy game,' I said to the man who was teaching me. 'Yes, most people find it easy at the beginning,' he replied drily. He was an old golfer himself; I thought he was jealous. I stuck well to the game, and for about three weeks I was immensely pleased with myself. Then, gradually, I began to find out the difficulties. I feel I shall never make a good player. Have you ever gone through that experience?"

"Yes," I replied; "I suppose that is the explanation. The game seems so easy at the beginning."

I left him to his lunch, and strolled westward, musing on the time when I should have answered that question of his about Christmas, or any other question, off-hand. That good youth time when I knew everything, when life presented no problems, dangled no doubts before me!

In those days, wishful to give the world the benefit of my wisdom, and seeking for a candlestick wherefrom my brilliancy might be visible and helpful unto men, I arrived before a dingy portal in Chequers Street, St. Luke's, behind which a conclave of young men, together with a few old enough to have known better, met every Friday evening for the purpose of discussing and arranging the affairs of the universe. "Speaking members" were charged ten-and-sixpence per annum, which must have worked out at an extremely moderate rate per word; and "gentlemen whose subscriptions were more than three months in arrear," became, by Rule seven, powerless for good or evil. We called ourselves "The Stormy Petrels," and, under the sympathetic shadow of those wings, I laboured two seasons towards the reformation of the human race; until, indeed, our treasurer, an earnest young man, and a tireless foe of all that was conventional, departed for the East, leaving behind him a balance sheet, showing that the club owed forty-two pounds fifteen and four-pence, and that the subscriptions for the current year, amounting to a little over thirty-eight pounds, had been "carried forward," but as to where, the report afforded no indication. Whereupon our landlord, a man utterly without ideals, seized our furniture, offering to sell it back to us for fifteen pounds. We pointed out to him that this was an extravagant price, and tendered him five.

The negotiations terminated with ungentlemanly language on his part, and "The Stormy Petrels" scattered, never to be foregathered together again above the troubled waters of humanity. Now-a-days, listening to the feeble plans of modern reformers, I cannot help but smile, remembering what was done in Chequers Street, St. Luke's, in an age when Mrs. Grundy still gave the law to literature, while yet the British matron was the guide to British art. I am informed that there is abroad the question of abolishing the House of Lords! Why, "The Stormy Petrels" abolished the aristocracy and the Crown in one evening, and then only adjourned for the purpose of appointing a committee to draw up and have ready a Republican Constitution by the following Friday evening. They talk of Empire lounges! We closed the doors of every music-hall in London eighteen years ago by twenty-nine votes to seventeen. They had a patient hearing, and were ably defended; but we found that the tendency of such amusements was anti-progressive, and against the best interests of an intellectually advancing democracy. I met the mover of the condemnatory resolution at the old "Pav" the following evening, and we continued the discussion over a bottle of Bass. He strengthened his argument by persuading me to sit out the whole of the three songs sung by the "Lion Comique"; but I subsequently retorted successfully, by bringing under his notice the dancing of a lady in blue tights and flaxen hair. I forget her name, but never shall I cease to remember her exquisite charm and beauty. Ah, me! how charming and how beautiful "artistes" were in those golden days! Whence have they vanished? Ladies in blue tights and flaxen hair dance before my eyes to- day, but move me not, unless it be towards boredom. Where be the tripping witches of twenty years ago, whom to see once was to dream of for a week, to touch whose white hand would have been joy, to kiss whose red lips would have been to foretaste Heaven. I heard only the other day that the son of an old friend of mine had secretly married a lady from the front row of the ballet, and involuntarily I exclaimed, "Poor devil!" There was a time when my first thought would have been, "Lucky beggar! is he worthy of her?" For then the ladies of the ballet were angels. How could one gaze at them – from the shilling pit – and doubt it? They danced to keep a widowed mother in comfort, or to send a younger brother to school. Then they were glorious creatures a young man did well to worship; but now-a-days –

It is an old jest. The eyes of youth see through rose-tinted glasses. The eyes of age are dim behind smoke-clouded spectacles. My flaxen friend, you are not the angel I dreamed you, nor the exceptional sinner some would paint you; but under your feathers, just a woman – a bundle of follies and failings, tied up with some sweetness and strength. You keep a brougham I am sure you cannot afford on your thirty shillings a week. There are ladies I know, in Mayfair, who have paid an extravagant price for theirs. You paint and you dye, I am told: it is even hinted you pad. Don't we all of us deck ourselves out in virtues that are not our own? When the paint and the powder, my sister, is stripped both from you and from me, we shall know which of us is entitled to look down on the other in scorn.

Forgive me, gentle Reader, for digressing. The lady led me astray. I was speaking of "The Stormy Petrels," and of the reforms they accomplished, which were many. We abolished, I remember, capital punishment and war; we were excellent young men at heart. Christmas we reformed altogether, along with Bank Holidays, by a majority of twelve. I never recollect any proposal to abolish anything ever being lost when put to the vote. There were few things that we "Stormy Petrels" did not abolish. We attacked Christmas on grounds of expediency, and killed it by ridicule. We exposed the hollow mockery of Christmas sentiment; we abused the indigestible Christmas dinner, the tiresome Christmas party, the silly Christmas pantomime. Our funny member was side-splitting on the subject of Christmas Waits; our social reformer bitter upon Christmas drunkenness; our economist indignant upon Christmas charities. Only one argument of any weight with us was advanced in favour of the festival, and that was our leading cynic's suggestion that it was worth enduring the miseries of Christmas, to enjoy the soul-satisfying comfort of the after reflection that it was all over, and could not occur again for another year.

But since those days when I was prepared to put this old world of ours to rights upon all matters, I have seen many sights and heard many sounds, and I am not quite so sure as I once was that my particular views are the only possibly correct ones. Christmas seems to me somewhat meaningless; but I have looked through windows in poverty-stricken streets, and have seen dingy parlours gay with many chains of coloured paper. They stretched from corner to corner of the smoke-grimed ceiling, they fell in clumsy festoons from the cheap gasalier, they framed the fly-blown mirror and the tawdry pictures; and I know tired hands and eyes worked many hours to fashion and fix those foolish chains, saying, "It will please him – she will like to see the room look pretty;" and as I have looked at them they have grown, in some mysterious manner, beautiful to me. The gaudy-coloured child and dog irritates me, I confess; but I have watched a grimy, inartistic personage, smoothing it affectionately with toil-stained hand, while eager faces crowded round to admire and wonder at its blatant crudity. It hangs to this day in its cheap frame above the chimney-piece, the one bright spot relieving those damp-stained walls; dull eyes stare and stare again at it, catching a vista, through its flashy tints, of the far-off land of art. Christmas Waits annoy me, and I yearn to throw open the window and fling coal at them – as once from the window of a high flat in Chelsea I did. I doubted their being genuine Waits. I was inclined to the opinion they were young men seeking excuse for making a noise. One of them appeared to know a hymn with a chorus, another played the concertina, while a third accompanied with a step dance. Instinctively I felt no respect for them; they disturbed me in my work, and the desire grew upon me to injure them. It occured to me it would be good sport if I turned out the light, softly opened the window, and threw coal at them. It would be impossible for them to tell from which window in the block the coal came, and thus subsequent unpleasantness would be avoided. They were a compact little group, and with average luck I was bound to hit one of them.

I adopted the plan. I could not see them very clearly. I aimed rather at the noise; and I had thrown about twenty choice lumps without effect, and was feeling somewhat discouraged, when a yell, followed by language singularly unappropriate to the season, told me that Providence had aided my arm. The music ceased suddenly, and the party dispersed, apparently in high glee – which struck me as curious.

One man I noticed remained behind. He stood under the lamp-post, and shook his fist at the block generally.

"Who threw that lump of coal?" he demanded in stentorian tones.

To my horror, it was the voice of the man at Eighty-eight, an Irish gentleman, a journalist like myself. I saw it all, as the unfortunate hero always exclaims, too late, in the play. He – number Eighty-eight – also disturbed by the noise, had evidently gone out to expostulate with the rioters. Of course my lump of coal had hit him – him the innocent, the peaceful (up till then), the virtuous. That is the justice Fate deals out to us mortals here below. There were ten to fourteen young men in that crowd, each one of whom fully deserved that lump of coal; he, the one guiltless, got it – seemingly, so far as the dim light from the gas lamp enabled me to judge, full in the eye.

As the block remained silent in answer to his demand, he crossed the road and mounted the stairs. On each landing he stopped and shouted –

"Who threw that lump of coal. I want the man who threw that lump of coal. Out you come."

Now a good man in my place would have waited till number Eighty-eight arrived on his landing, and then, throwing open the door, would have said with manly candour –

"*I* threw that lump of coal. I was –," He would not have got further, because at that point, I feel confident, number Eighty-eight would have punched his head. There would have been an unseemly fracas on the staircase, to the annoyance of all the other tenants; and later, there would have issued a summons and a cross-summons. Angry passions would have been roused, bitter feeling engendered which might have lasted for years.

I do not pretend to be a good man. I doubt if the pretence would be of any use were I to try: I am not a sufficiently good actor. I said to myself, as I took off my boots in the study, preparatory to retiring to my bedroom – "Number Eighty-eight is evidently not in a frame of mind to listen to my story. It will be better to let him shout himself cool; after which he will return to his own flat, bathe his eye, and obtain some refreshing sleep. In the morning, when we shall probably meet as usual on our way to Fleet Street, I will refer to the incident casually, and sympathize with him. I will suggest to him the truth – that in all probability some fellow-tenant, irritated also by the noise, had aimed coal at the Waits, hitting him instead by a regrettable but pure accident. With tact I may even be able to make him see the humour of the incident. Later on, in March or April, choosing my moment with judgment, I will, perhaps, confess that I was that fellow-tenant, and over a friendly brandy-and-soda we will laugh the whole trouble away."

As a matter of fact, that is what happened. Said number Eighty-eight – he was a big man, as good a fellow at heart as ever lived, but impulsive – "Damned lucky for you, old man, you did not tell me at the time."

"I felt," I replied, "instinctively that it was a case for delay."

There are times when one should control one's passion for candour; and as I was saying, Christmas Waits excite no emotion in my breast save that of irritation. But I have known "Hark, the herald angels sing," wheezily chanted by fog-filled throats, and accompanied, hopelessly out of time, by a cornet and a flute, bring a great look of gladness to a work-worn face. To her it was a message of hope and love, making the hard life taste sweet. The mere thought of family gatherings, so customary at Christmas time, bores us superior people; but I think of an incident told me by a certain man, a friend of mine. One Christmas, my friend, visiting in the country, came face to face with a woman whom in town he had often met amid very different surroundings. The door of the little farmhouse was open; she and an older woman were ironing at a table, and as her soft white hands passed to and fro, folding and smoothing the rumpled heap, she laughed and talked, concerning simple homely things. My friend's shadow fell across her work, and she, looking up, their eyes met; but her face said plainly, "I do not know you here, and here you do not know me. Here I am a woman loved and respected." My friend passed in and spoke to the older woman, the wife of one of his host's tenants, and she turned towards, and introduced the younger – "My daughter, sir. We do not see her very often. She is in a place in London, and cannot get away. But she always spends a few days with us at Christmas."

"It is the season for family re-unions," answered my friend with just the suggestion of a sneer, for which he hated himself.

"Yes, sir," said the woman, not noticing; "she has never missed her Christmas with us, have you, Bess?"

"No, mother," replied the girl simply, and bent her head again over her work.

So for these few days every year this woman left her furs and jewels, her fine clothes and dainty foods, behind her, and lived for a little space with what was clean and wholesome. It was the one anchor holding her to womanhood; and one likes to think that it was, perhaps, in the end strong enough to save her from the drifting waters. All which arguments in favour of Christmas and of Christmas customs are, I admit, purely sentimental ones, but I have lived long enough to doubt whether sentiment has not its legitimate place in the economy of life.

TIME WASTED IN LOOKING
BEFORE ONE LEAPS

Have you ever noticed the going out of a woman?

When a man goes out, he says – "I'm going out, shan't be long."

"Oh, George," cries his wife from the other end of the house, "don't go for a moment. I want you to –" She hears a falling of hats, followed by the slamming of the front door.

"Oh, George, you're not gone!" she wails. It is but the voice of despair. As a matter of fact, she knows he is gone. She reaches the hall, breathless.

"He might have waited a minute," she mutters to herself, as she picks up the hats, "there were so many things I wanted him to do."

She does not open the door and attempt to stop him, she knows he is already half-way down the street. It is a mean, paltry way of going out, she thinks; so like a man.

When a woman, on the other hand, goes out, people know about it. She does not sneak out. She says she is going out. She says it, generally, on the afternoon of the day before; and she repeats it, at intervals, until tea-time. At tea, she suddenly decides that she won't, that she will leave it till the day after to-morrow instead. An hour later she thinks she will go to-morrow, after all, and makes arrangements to wash her hair over-night. For the next hour or so she alternates between fits of exaltation, during which she looks forward to going out, and moments of despondency, when a sense of foreboding falls upon her. At dinner she persuades some other woman to go with her; the other woman, once persuaded, is enthusiastic about going, until she recollects that she cannot. The first woman, however, convinces her that she can.

"Yes," replies the second woman, "but then, how about you, dear? You are forgetting the Joneses."

"So I was," answers the first woman, completely nonplussed. "How very awkward, and I can't go on Wednesday. I shall have to leave it till Thursday, now."

"But *I* can't go Thursday," says the second woman.

"Well, you go without me, dear," says the first woman, in the tone of one who is sacrificing a life's ambition.

"Oh no, dear, I should not think of it," nobly exclaims the second woman. "We will wait and go together, Friday."

"I'll tell you what we'll do," says the first woman. "We will start early" (this is an inspiration), "and be back before the Joneses arrive."

They agree to sleep together; there is a lurking suspicion in both their minds that this may be their last sleep on earth. They retire early with a can of hot water. At intervals, during the night, one overhears them splashing water, and talking.

They come down very late for breakfast, and both very cross. Each seems to have argued herself into the belief that she has been lured into this piece of nonsense, against her better judgment, by the persistent folly of the other one. During the meal each one asks the other, every five minutes, if she is quite ready. Each one, it appears, has only her hat to put on. They talk about the weather, and wonder what it is going to do. They wish it would make up its mind, one way or the other. They are very bitter on weather that cannot make up its mind. After breakfast it still looks cloudy, and they decide to abandon the scheme altogether. The first woman then remembers that it is absolutely necessary for her, at all events, to go.

"But there is no need for you to come, dear," she says.

Up to that point the second woman was evidently not sure whether she wished to go or whether she didn't. Now she knows.

"Oh yes, I'll come," she says, "then it will be over."

"I am sure you don't want to go," urges the first woman, "and I shall be quicker by myself. I am ready to start now."

The second woman bridles.

"*I* shan't be a couple of minutes," she retorts. "You know, dear, it's generally *I* who have to wait for *you*."

"But you've not got your boots on," the first woman reminds her.

"Well, they won't take *any* time," is the answer. "But of course, dear, if you'd really rather I did not come, say so." By this time she is on the verge of tears.

"Of course, I would like you to come, dear," explains the first in a resigned tone. "I thought perhaps you were only coming to please me."

"Oh no, I'd *like* to come," says the second woman.

"Well, we must hurry up," says the first; "I shan't be more than a minute myself. I've merely got to change my skirt."

Half-an-hour later you hear them calling to each other, from different parts of the house, to know if the other one is ready. It appears they have both been ready for quite a long while, waiting only for the other one.

"I'm afaid," calls out the one whose turn it is to be down-stairs, "it's going to rain."

"Oh, don't say that," calls back the other one.

"Well, it looks very like it."

"What a nuisance," answers the up-stairs woman; "shall we put it off?"

"Well, what do *you* think, dear?" replies the down-stairs.

They decide they will go, only now they will have to change their boots, and put on different hats.

For the next ten minutes they are still shouting and running about. Then it seems as if they really were ready, nothing remaining but for them to say "Good-bye," and go.

They begin by kissing the children. A woman never leaves her house without secret misgivings that she will never return to it alive. One child cannot be found. When it is found it wishes it hadn't been. It has to be washed, preparatory to being kissed. After that, the dog has to be found and kissed, and final instructions given to the cook.

Then they open the front door.

"Oh, George," calls out the first woman, turning round again. "Are you there?"

"Hullo," answers a voice from the distance. "Do you want me?"

"No, dear, only to say good-bye. I'm going."

"Oh, good-bye."

"Good-bye, dear. Do you think it's going to rain?"

"Oh no, I should not say so."

"George."

"Yes."

"Have you got any money?"

Five minutes later they come running back; the one has forgotten her parasol, the other her purse.

And speaking of purses, reminds one of another essential difference between the male and female human animal. A man carries his money in his pocket. When he wants to use it, he takes it out and lays it down. This is a crude way of doing things, a woman displays more subtlety. Say she is standing in the street, and wants fourpence to pay for a bunch of violets she has purchased from a flower-girl. She has two parcels in one hand, and a parasol in the other. With the remaining two fingers of the left hand she secures the violets. The question then arises, how to pay the girl? She flutters for a few minutes, evidently not quite understanding why it is she cannot do it. The reason then occurs to her: she has only two hands

and both these are occupied. First she thinks she will put
the parcels and the flowers into her right hand, then she
thinks she will put the parasol into her left. Then she
looks round for a table or even a chair, but there is not
such a thing in the whole street. Her difficulty is solved
by her dropping the parcels and the flowers. The girl
picks them up for her and holds them. This enables her
to feel for her pocket with her right hand, while waving
her open parasol about with her left. She knocks an old
gentleman's hat off into the gutter, and nearly blinds the
flower-girl before it occurs to her to close it. This done,
she leans it up against the flower-girl's basket, and sets to
work in earnest with both hands. She seizes herself firmly
by the back, and turns the upper part of her body round
till her hair is in front and her eyes behind. Still holding
herself firmly with her left hand – did she let herself go,
goodness knows where she would spin to; – with her
right she prospects herself. The purse is there, she can
feel it, the problem is how to get at it. The quickest way
would, of course, be to take off the skirt, sit down on the
kerb, turn it inside out, and work from the bottom of the
pocket upwards. But this simple idea never seems to
occur to her. There are some thirty folds at the back of
the dress, between two of these folds commences the
secret passage. At last, purely by chance, she suddenly
discovers it, nearly upsetting herself in the process, and
the purse is brought up to the surface. The difficulty of
opening it still remains. She knows it opens with a
spring, but the secret of that spring she has never
mastered, and she never will. Her plan is to worry it
generally until it does open. Five minutes will always do
it, provided she is not flustered.

At last it does open. It would be incorrect to say that
she opens it. It opens because it is sick of being mauled
about; and, as likely as not, it opens at the moment when
she is holding it upside down. If you happen to be near
enough to look over her shoulder, you will notice that the
gold and silver lies loose within it. In an inner sanctuary,

carefully secured with a second secret spring, she keeps her coppers, together with a postage stamp and a draper's receipt, nine months old, for elevenpence three-farthings.

I remember the indignation of an old Bus-conductor, once. Inside we were nine women and two men. I sat next the door, and his remarks therefore he addressed to me. It was certainly taking him some time to collect the fares, but I think he would have got on better had he been less bustling; he worried them, and made them nervous.

"Look at that," he said, drawing my attention to a poor lady opposite, who was diving in the customary manner for her purse, "they sit on their money, women do. Blest if you wouldn't think they was trying to 'atch it."

At length the lady drew from underneath herself an exceedingly fat purse.

"Fancy riding in a bumpy bus, perched up on that thing," he continued. "Think what a stamina they must have." He grew confidential. "I've seen one woman," he said, "pull out from underneath 'er a street door-key, a tin box of lozengers, a pencil-case, a whopping big purse, a packet of hair-pins, and a smelling-bottle. Why, you or me would be wretched, sitting on a plain door-knob, and them women goes about like that all day. I suppose they gets used to it. Drop 'em on an eider-down pillow, and they'd scream. The time it takes me to get tuppence out of them, why, it's 'eart-breaking. First they tries one side, then they tries the other. Then they gets up and shakes theirselves till the bus jerks them back again, and there they are, a more 'opeless 'eap than ever. If I 'ad my way I'd make every bus carry a female searcher as could over'aul 'em one at a time, and take the money from 'em. Talk about the poor pickpocket. What I say is, that a man as finds his way into a woman's pocket – well, he deserves what he gets."

But it was the thought of more serious matters that lured me into reflections concerning the over-carefulness

of women. It is a theory of mine – wrong possibly; indeed
I have so been informed – that we pick our way through
life with too much care. We are for ever looking down
upon the ground. Maybe, we do avoid a stumble or two
over a stone or a brier, but also we miss the blue of the
sky, the glory of the hills. These books that good men
write, telling us that what they call "success" in life
depends on our flinging aside our youth and wasting our
manhood in order that we may have the means when we
are eighty of spending a rollicking old age, annoy me. We
save all our lives to invest in a South Sea Bubble; and in
skimping and scheming, we have grown mean, and
narrow, and hard. We will put off the gathering of the
roses till to-morrow, to-day it shall be all work, all
bargain-driving, all plotting. Lo, when to-morrow
comes, the roses are blown; nor do we care for roses, idle
things of small marketable value; cabbages are more to
our fancy by the time to-morrow comes.

Life is a thing to be lived, not spent, to be faced, not
ordered. Life is not a game of chess, the victory to the
most knowing; it is a game of cards, one's hand by skill to
be made the best of. Is it the wisest who is always the
most successful? I think not. The luckiest whist-player I
ever came across was a man who was never *quite* certain
what were trumps, and who most frequent observation
during the game was "I really beg your pardon,"
addressed to his partner; a remark which generally
elicited the reply, "Oh, don't apologize. All's well that
ends well." The man I knew who made the most rapid
fortune was a builder in the outskirts of Birmingham,
who could not write his name, and who, for thirty years
of his life, never went to bed sober. I do not say that
forgetfulness of trumps should be cultivated by
whist-players. I think my builder friend might have been
even more successful had he learned to write his name,
and had he occasionally – not overdoing it – enjoyed a
sober evening. All I wish to impress is, that virtue is not
the road to success – of the kind we are dealing with. We

must find other reasons for being virtuous; maybe, there are some. The truth is, life is a gamble pure and simple, and the rules we lay down for success are akin to the infallible systems with which a certain class of idiot goes armed each season to Monte Carlo. We can play the game with coolness and judgment, decide when to plunge and when to stake small; but to think that wisdom will decide it, is to imagine that we have discovered the law of chance. Let us play the game of life as sportsmen, pocketing our winnings with a smile, leaving our losings with a shrug. Perhaps that is why we have been summoned to the board and the cards dealt round: that we may learn some of the virtues of the good gambler; his self-control, his courage under misfortune, his modesty under the strain of success, his firmness, his alertness, his general indifference to fate. Good lessons these, all of them. If by the game we learn some of them our time on the green earth has not been wasted. If we rise from the table having learned only fretfulness and self-pity I fear it has been.

The grim Hall Porter taps at the door: "Number Five hundred billion and twenty-eight, your boatman is waiting, sir."

So! is it time already? We pick up our counters. Of what use are they? In the country the other side of the river they are no tender. The blood-red for gold, and the pale-green for love, to whom shall we fling them? Here is some poor beggar longing to play, let us give them to him as we pass out. Poor devil! the game will amuse him – for a while.

Keep your powder dry, and trust in Providence, is the motto of the wise. Wet powder could never be of any possible use to you. Dry, it may be, *with* the help of Providence. We will call it Providence, it is a prettier name than Chance – perhaps also a truer.

Another mistake we make when we reason out our lives is this: we reason as though we were planning for reasonable creatures. It is a big mistake. Well-meaning ladies and gentlemen make it when they picture their ideal worlds. When marriage is reformed, and the social problem solved, when poverty and war have been abolished by acclamation, and sin and sorrow rescinded by an over-whelming parliamentary majority! Ah, then the world will be worthy of our living in it. You need not wait, ladies and gentlemen, so long as you think for that time. No social revolution is needed, no slow education of the people is necessary. It would all come about to-morrow, *if only we were reasonable creatures*.

Imagine a world of reasonable beings! The Ten Commandments would be unnecessary: no reasoning being sins, no reasoning creature makes mistakes. There would be no rich men, for what reasonable man cares for luxury and ostentation? There would be no poor: that I should eat enough for two while my brother in the next street, as good a man as I, starves, is not reasonable. There would be no difference of opinion on any two points: there is only one reason. You, dear Reader, would find, that on all subjects you were of the same opinion as I. No novels would be written, no plays performed; the lives of reasonable creatures do not afford drama. No mad loves, no mad laughter, no scalding tears, no fierce unreasoning, brief-lived joys, no sorrows, no wild dreams – only reason, reason everywhere.

But for the present we remain unreasonable. If I eat this mayonnaise, drink this champagne, I shall suffer in my liver. Then, why do I eat it? Julia is a charming girl, amiable, wise, and witty; also she has a share in a brewery. Then, why does John marry Ann? who is short-tempered, to say the least of it, who, he feels, will not make him so good a house-wife, who has extravagant notions, who has no little fortune. There is something about Ann's chin that fascinates him – he could not explain to you what. On the whole, Julia is the better-looking of the two. But the more he thinks of Julia, the more he is drawn towards Ann. So Tom marries Julia, and the brewery fails, and Julia, on a holiday, contracts rheumatic fever, and is a helpless invalid for life; while Ann comes in for ten thousand pounds left to her by an Australian uncle no one had ever heard of.

I have been told of a young man, who chose his wife with excellent care. Said he to himself, very wisely, "In the selection of a wife a man cannot be too circumspect." He convinced himself that the girl was everything a helpmate should be. She had every virtue that could be expected in a woman, no faults, but such as are inseparable from a woman. Speaking practically, she was perfection. He married her, and found she was all he had thought her. Only one thing could he urge against her – that he did not like her. And that, of course, was not her fault.

How easy life would be did we know ourselves. Could we always be sure that to-morrow we should think as we do to-day. We fall in love during a summer holiday; she is fresh, delightful, altogether charming; the blood rushes to our head every time we think of her. Our ideal career is one of perpetual service at her feet. It seems impossible that Fate could bestow upon us any greater happiness than the privilege of cleaning her boots, and kissing the hem of her garment – if the hem be a little muddy that will please us the more. We tell her our ambition, and at that moment every word we utter is sincere. But the summer holiday passes, and with it the holiday mood, and winter finds us wondering how we are going to get out of the difficulty into which we have landed ourselves. Or worse still, perhaps, the mood lasts longer than is usual. We become formally engaged. We marry – I wonder how many marriages are the result of a passion that is burnt out before the altar-rails are reached? – and three months afterwards the little lass is broken-hearted to find that we consider the lacing of her boots a bore. Her feet seem to have grown bigger. There is no excuse for us, save that we are silly children, never sure of what we are crying for, hurting one another in our play, crying very loudly when hurt ourselves.

I knew an American lady once who used to bore me with long accounts of the brutalities exercised upon her by her husband. She had instituted divorce proceedings against him. The trial came on, and she was highly successful. We all congratulated her, and then for some months she dropped out of my life. But there came a day when we again found ourselves together. One of the problems of social life is to know what to say to one another when we meet; every man and woman's desire is to appear sympathetic and clever, and this makes conversation difficult, because, taking us all round, we are neither sympathetic nor clever – but this by the way. Of course, I began to talk to her about her former husband. I asked her how he was getting on. She replied that she thought he was very comfortable.

"Married again?" I suggested.

"Yes," she answered.

"Serve him right," I exclaimed, "and his wife too." She was a pretty, bright-eyed little woman, my American friend, and I wished to ingratiate myself. "A woman who would marry such a man, knowing what she must have known of him, is sure to make him wretched, and we may trust him to be a curse to her."

My friend seemed inclined to defend him.

"I think he is greatly improved," she argued.

"Nonsense!" I returned, "a man never improves. Once a villain, always a villain."

"Oh, hush!" she pleaded, "you mustn't call him that."

"Why not?" I answered. "I have heard you call him a villain yourself."

"It was wrong of me," she said, flushing. "I'm afraid he was not the only one to be blamed; we were both foolish in those days, but I think we have both learned a lesson."

I remained silent, waiting for the necessary explanation.

"You had better come and see him for yourself," she added, with a little laugh; "to tell the truth, I am the woman who has married him. Tuesday is my day, Number 2, K—— Mansions," and she ran off, leaving me staring after her.

I believe an enterprising clergyman who would set up a little church in the Strand, just outside the Law Courts, might do quite a trade, re-marrying couples who had just been divorced. A friend of mine, a respondent, told me he had never loved his wife more than on two occasions – the first when she refused him, the second when she came into the witness-box to give evidence against him.

"You are curious creatures, you men," remarked a lady once to another man in my presence. "You never seem to know your own mind."

She was feeling annoyed with men generally. I do not blame her, I feel annoyed with them myself sometimes. There is one man in particular I am always feeling intensely irritated against. He says one thing, and acts another. He will talk like a saint and behave like a fool, knows what is right and does what is wrong. But we will not speak further of him. He will be all he should be one day, and then we will pack him into a nice, comfortably-lined box, and screw the lid down tight upon him, and put him away in a quiet little spot near a church I know of, lest he should get up and misbehave himself again.

The other man, who is a wise man as men go, looked at his fair critic with a smile.

"My dear madam," he replied, "you are blaming the wrong person. I confess I do not know my mind, and what little I do know of it I do not like. I did not make it, I did not select it. I am more dissatisfied with it than you can possibly be. It is a greater mystery to me than it is to you, and I have to live with it. You should pity not blame me."

There are moods in which I fall to envying those old hermits who frankly, and with courageous cowardice, shirked the problem of life. There are days when I dream of an existence unfettered by the thousand petty strings with which our souls lie bound to Lilliputia land. I picture myself living in some Norwegian sater, high above the black waters of a rock-bound fiord. No other human creature disputes with me my kingdom. I am alone with the whispering fir forests and the stars. How I live I am not quite sure. Once a month I could journey down into the villages and return laden. I should not need much. For the rest, my gun and fishing-rod would supply me. I would have with me a couple of big dogs, who would talk to me with their eyes, so full of dumb thought, and together we would wander over the uplands, seeking our dinner, after the old primitive fashion of the men who dreamt not of ten-course dinners and Savoy suppers. I would cook the food myself, and sit down to the meal with a bottle of good wine, such as starts a man's thoughts (for I am inconsistent, as I acknowledge, and that gift of civilization I would bear with me into my hermitage). Then in the evening, with pipe in mouth, beside my log-wood fire, I would sit and think, until new knowledge came to me. Strengthened by those silent voices that are drowned in the roar of Streetland, I might, perhaps, grow into something nearer to what it was intended that a man should be – might catch a glimpse, perhaps, of the meaning of life.

No, no, my dear lady, into this life of renunciation I would not take a companion, certainly not of the sex you are thinking of, even would she care to come, which I doubt. There are times when a man is better without the woman, when a woman is better without the man. Love drags us from the depths, makes men and women of us, but if we would climb a little nearer to the stars we must say good-bye to it. We men and women do not show ourselves to each other at our best; too often, I fear, at our worst. The woman's highest ideal of man is the lover; to a man the woman is always the possible beloved. We see each other's hearts, but not each other's souls. In each other's presence we never shake ourselves free from the earth. Match-making mother Nature is always at hand to prompt us. A woman lifts us up into manhood, but there she would have us stay. "Climb up to me," she cries to the lad, walking with soiled feet in muddy ways; "be a true man that you may be worthy to walk by my side; be brave to protect me, kind, and tender, and true; but climb no higher, stay here by my side." The martyr, the prophet, the leader of the world's forlorn hopes, she would wake from his dream. Her arms she would fling about his neck holding him down.

To the woman the man says, "You are my wife. Here is your America, within these walls, here is your work, your duty." True, in nine hundred and ninety-nine cases out of every thousand, but men and women are not made in moulds, and the world's work is various. Sometimes to her sorrow, a woman's work lies beyond the home. The duty of Mary was not to Joseph.

The hero in the popular novel is the young man who says, "I love you better than my soul." Our favourite heroine in fiction is the woman who cries to her lover, "I would go down into Hell to be with you." There are men and women who cannot answer thus – the men who dream dreams, the women who see visions – impracticable people from the Bayswater point of view. But Bayswater would not be the abode of peace it is had it not been for such.

Have we not placed sexual love on a pedestal higher than it deserves? It is a noble passion, but it is not the noblest. There is a wider love by the side of which it is but as the lamp illumining the cottage, to the moonlight bathing the hills and valleys. There were two women once. This is a play I saw acted in the daylight. They had been friends from girlhood, till there came between them the usual trouble – a man. A weak, pretty creature not worth a thought from either of them; but women love the unworthy; there would be no over-population problem did they not; and this poor specimen, ill-luck had ordained they should contend for.

Their rivalry brought out all that was worst in both of them. It is a mistake to suppose love only elevates; it can debase. It was a mean struggle for what to an onlooker must have appeared a remarkably unsatisfying prize. The loser might well have left the conqueror to her poor triumph, even granting it had been gained unfairly. But the old, ugly, primeval passions had been stirred in these women, and the wedding-bells closed only the first act.

The second is not difficult to guess. It would have ended in the Divorce Court had not the deserted wife felt that a finer revenge would be secured to her by silence.

In the third, after an interval of only eighteen months, the man died – the first piece of good fortune that seems to have occurred to him personally throughout the play. His position must have been an exceedingly anxious one from the beginning. Notwithstanding his flabbiness, one cannot but regard him with a certain amount of pity – not unmixed with amusement. Most of life's dramas can be viewed as either farce or tragedy according to the whim of the spectator. The actors invariably play them as tragedy; but then that is the essence of good farce acting.

Thus was secured the triumph of legal virtue and the punishment of irregularity, and the play might be dismissed as uninterestingly orthodox were it not for the fourth act, showing how the wronged wife came to the woman she had once wronged to ask and grant forgiveness. Strangely as it may sound, they found their love for one another unchanged. They had been long parted: it was sweet to hold each other's hands again. Two lonely women, they agreed to live together. Those who knew them well in this later time say that their life was very beautiful, filled with graciousness and nobility.

I do not say that such a story could ever be common, but it is more probable than the world might credit. Sometimes the man is better without the woman, the woman without the man.

ON THE NOBILITY OF OURSELVES

An old Anglicized Frenchman, I used to meet often in my earlier journalistic days, held a theory, concerning man's future state, that has since come to afford me more food for reflection than, at the time I should have deemed possible. He was a bright-eyed, eager little man. One felt no Lotus land could be Paradise to him. We build our heaven of the stones of our desires: to the old, red-bearded Norseman, a foe to fight and a cup to drain; to the artistic Greek, a grove of animated statuary; to the Red Indian, his happy hunting ground; to the Turk, his harem; to the Jew, his New Jerusalem, paved with gold; to others, according to their taste, limited by the range of their imagination.

Few things had more terrors for me, when a child, than Heaven – as pictured for me by certain of the good folks round about me. I was told that if I were a good lad, kept my hair tidy, and did not tease the cat, I would probably, when I died, go to a place where all day long I would sit still and sing hymns. (Think of it! as reward to a healthy boy for being good.) There would be no breakfast and no dinner, no tea and no supper. One old lady cheered me a little with a hint that the monotony might be broken by a little manna; but the idea of everlasting manna palled upon me, and my suggestions, concerning the possibilities of sherbet or jumbles, were scouted as irreverent. There would be no school, but also there would be no cricket and no rounders. I should feel no desire, so I was assured, to do another angel's "dags" by sliding down the heavenly banisters. My only joy would be to sing.

"Shall we start singing the moment we get up in the morning?" I asked.

"There won't be any morning," was the answer. "There will be no day and no night. It will all be one long day without end."

"And shall we always be singing?" I persisted.

"Yes, you will be so happy, you will always want to sing."

"Shan't I ever get tired?"

"No, you will never get tired, and you will never get sleepy or hungry or thirsty."

"And does it go on like that for ever?"

"Yes, for ever and ever."

"Will it go on for a million years?"

"Yes, a million years, and then another million years, and then another million years after that. There will never be any end to it."

I can remember to this day the agony of those nights, when I would lie awake, thinking of this endless heaven, from which there seemed to be no possible escape. For the other place was equally eternal, or I might have been tempted to seek refuge there.

We grown up folk, our brains dulled by the slowly acquired habit of not thinking, do wrong to torture children with these awful themes. Eternity, Heaven, Hell are meaningless words to use. We repeat them, as we gabble our prayers, telling our smug, self-satisfied selves that we are miserable sinners. But to the child, the "intelligent stranger" in the land, seeking to know, they are fearful realities. If you doubt me, Reader, stand by yourself, beneath the stars, one night, and *solve* this thought, Eternity. Your next address shall be the County Lunatic Asylum.

My actively inclined French friend held cheerier views than are common of man's life beyond the grave. His belief was that we were destined to constant change, to everlasting work. We were to pass through the older planets, to labour in the greater suns.

But for such advanced career a more capable being was needed. No one of us was sufficient, he argued, to be granted a future existence all to himself. His idea was that two or three or four of us, according to our intrinsic value, would be combined to make a new and more important individuality, fitted for a higher existence. Man, he pointed out, was already a collection of the beasts. "You and I," he, would say, tapping first my chest and then his own, "we have them all here – the ape, the tiger, the pig, the motherly hen, the gamecock, the good ant; we are all, rolled into one. So the man of the future, he will be made up of many men – the courage of one, the wisdom of another, the kindliness of a third."

"Take a City man," he would continue, "say the Lord Mayor; add to him a poet, say Swinburne; mix them with a religious enthusiast, say General Booth. There you will have the man fit for the higher life."

Garibaldi and Bismarck, he held, should make a very fine mixture, correcting one another; if needful, extract of Ibsen might be added, as seasoning. He thought that Irish politicians would mix admirably with Scotch divines; that Oxford Dons would go well with lady novelists. He was convinced that Count Tolstoi, a few Gaiety Johnnies (we called them "mashers" in those days,) together with a humourist – he was kind enough to suggest myself – would produce something very choice. Queen Elizabeth, he fancied, was probably being reserved to go – let us hope in the long distant future – with Ouida. It sounds a whimsical theory, set down here in my words, not his; but the old fellow was so much in earnest that few of us ever thought to laugh as he talked. Indeed, there were moments on starry nights, as walking home from the office, we would pause on Waterloo

Bridge to enjoy the witchery of the long line of the Embankment lights, when I could almost believe, as I listened to him, in the not impossibility of his dreams.

Even as regards this world, it would often be a gain, one thinks, and no loss, if some half-dozen of us were rolled together, or boiled down, or whatever the process necessary might be, and something made out of us in that way.

Have not you, my fair Reader, sometimes thought to yourself what a delightful husband Tom this, plus Harry that, plus Dick the other, would make? Tom is always so cheerful and good-tempered, yet you feel that in the serious moments of life he would be lacking. A delightful hubby when you felt merry, yes; but you would not go to him for comfort and strength in your troubles, now would you? No, in your hour of sorrow, how good it would be to have near you grave, earnest Harry. He is a "good sort," Harry. Perhaps, after all, he is the best of the three – solid, staunch, and true. What a pity he is just a trifle commonplace and unambitious. Your friends, not knowing his sterling hidden qualities, would hardly envy you; and a husband that no other girl envies you – well, that would hardly be satisfactory, would it? Dick, on the other hand, is clever and brilliant. He will make his way; there will come a day, you are convinced, when a woman will be proud to bear his name. If only he were not so self-centred, if only he were more sympathetic.

But a combination of the three, or rather of the best qualities of the three – Tom's good temper, Harry's tender strength, Dick's brilliant masterfulness: that is the man who would be worthy of you.

The woman David Copperfield wanted was Agnes and Dora rolled into one. He had to take them one after the other, which was not so nice. And did he really love Agnes, Mr. Dickens; or merely feel he ought to? Forgive me, but I am doubtful concerning that second marriage of Copperfield's. Come, strictly between ourselves, Mr. Dickens, was not David, good human soul! now and again a wee bit bored by the immaculate Agnes? She made him an excellent wife, I am sure. *She* never ordered oysters by the barrel, unopened. It would, on any day, have been safe to ask Traddles home to dinner; in fact, Sophie and the whole rose-garden might have accompanied him, Agnes would have been equal to the occasion. The dinner would have been perfectly cooked and served, and Agnes' sweet smile would have pervaded the meal. But *after* the dinner, when David and Traddles sat smoking alone, while from the drawing- room drifted down the notes of high-class, elevating music, played by the saintly Agnes, did they never, glancing covertly towards the empty chair between them, see the laughing, curl-framed face of a very foolish little woman – one of those foolish little women that a wise man thanks God for making – and wish, in spite of all, that it were flesh and blood, not shadow?

Oh, you foolish wise folk, who would remodel human nature! Cannot you see how great is the work given unto childish hands? Think you that in well-ordered housekeeping and high-class conversation lies the whole making of a man? Foolish Dora, fashioned by clever old magician Nature, who knows that weakness and helplessness are as a talisman calling forth strength and tenderness in man, trouble yourself not unduly about those oysters nor the underdone mutton, little woman. Good plain cooks at twenty pounds a year will see to these things for us; and, now and then, when a windfall comes our way, we will dine together at a moderate- priced restaurant where these things are managed even better. Your work, Dear, is to teach us gentleness and kindliness. Lay your curls here, child. It is from such as you that we learn wisdom. Foolish wise folk sneer as you; foolish wise folk would pull up the useless lilies, the needless roses, from the garden, would plant in their places only serviceable wholesome cabbage. But the Gardener, knowing better, plants the silly short-lived flowers; foolish wise folk, asking for what purpose.

As for Agnes, Mr. Dickens, do you know what she always makes me think of? You will not mind my saying? – the woman one reads about. Frankly, I don't believe in her. I do not refer to Agnes in particular, but the woman of whom she is a type, the faultless woman we read of. Women have many faults, but, thank God, they have one redeeming virtue – they are none of them faultless.

But the heroine of fiction! oh, a terrible dragon of virtue is she. May heaven preserve us poor men, undeserving though we be, from a life with the heroine of fiction. She is all soul, and heart, and intellect, with never a bit of human nature to catch hold of her by. Her beauty, it appals one, it is so painfully indescribable. Whence comes she, whither goes she, why do we never meet her like? Of women I know a goodish few, and I look among them for her prototype; but I find it not. They are charming, they are beautiful, all these women that I know. It would not be right for me to tell you, Ladies, the esteem and veneration with which I regard you all. You yourselves, blushing, would be the first to check my ardour. But yet, dear Ladies, seen even through me eyes, you come not near the ladies that I read about. You are not – if I may be permitted an expressive vulgarism – in the same street with them. Your beauty I can look upon, and retain my reason – for whatever value that may be to me. Your conversation, I admit, is clever and brilliant in the extreme; your knowledge vast and various; your culture quite Bostonian; yet you do not – I hardly know how to express it – you do not shine with the sixteen full-moon-power of the heroine of fiction. You do not – and I thank you for it – impress me with the idea that you are the only women on earth. You, even you, possess tempers of your own. I am inclined to think you take an interest in your clothes. I would not be sure, even, that you do not mingle a little of "your own hair" (you know what I mean) with the hair of your head.

There is in your temperament a vein of vanity, a suggestion of selfishness, a spice of laziness. I have known you a trifle unreasonable, a little inconsiderate, slightly exacting. Unlike the heroine of fiction, you have a certain number of human appetites and instincts; a few human follies, perhaps, a human fault, or shall we say two? In short, dear Ladies, you also, even as we men, are the children of Adam and Eve. Tell me, if you know, where I may meet with this supernatural sister of yours, this woman that one reads about. She never keeps any one waiting while she does her back hair, she is never indignant with everybody else in the house because she cannot find her own boots, she never scolds the servants, she is never cross with the children, she never slams the door, she is never jealous of her younger sister, she never lingers at the gate with any cousin but the right one.

Dear me, where *do* they keep them, these women that one reads about? I suppose where they keep the pretty girl of Art. You have seen her, have you not, Reader, the pretty girl in the picture? She leaps the six-barred gate with a yard and a half to spare, turning round in her saddle the while to make some smiling remark to the comic man behind, who, of course, is standing on his head in the ditch. She floats gracefully off Dieppe on stormy mornings. Her *baignoire* – generally of chiffon and old point lace – has not lost a curve. The older ladies, bathing round her, look wet. Their dress clings damply to their limbs. But the pretty girl of Art dives, and never a curl of her hair is disarranged. The pretty girl of Art stands lightly on tip-toe and volleys a tennis-ball six feet above her head. The pretty girl of Art keeps the head of the punt straight against a stiff current and a strong wind. *She* never gets the water up her sleeve, and down her back, and all over the cushions. *Her* pole never sticks in the mud, with the steam launch ten yards off and the man looking the other way. The pretty girl of Art skates in high-heeled French shoes at an angle of forty-five to the surface of the ice, both hands in her muff. *She* never sits down plump, with her feet a yard apart, and says, "Ough." The pretty girl of Art drives tandem down Piccadilly, during the height of the season, at eighteen miles an hour. It never occurs to *her* leader that the time has now arrived for him to turn round and get into the cart. The pretty girl of Art rides her bicycle through the town on market day, carrying a basket of eggs, and smiling right and left. *She* never throws away both her handles and runs into a cow. The pretty girl of Art goes trout fishing in open-work stockings, under a blazing sun, with a bunch of dew-bespangled primroses in her hair; and every time she gracefully flicks her rod she hauls out a salmon. *She* never ties herself up to a tree, or hooks the dog. *She* never comes home, soaked and disagreeable, to tell you that she caught six, but put them all back again, because they were merely two or three-pounders, and not worth the trouble of carrying. The pretty girl of Art plays croquet with one hand, and looks as if she enjoyed the game. *She* never tries to accidentally kick her ball into position when nobody is noticing, or stands it out that she is through a hoop that she knows she isn't.

She is a good, all-round sprtswoman, is the pretty girl in the picture. The only thing I have to say against her is that she makes one dissatisfied with the girl out of the picture – the girl who mistakes a punt for a teetotum, so that you land feeling as if you had had a day in the Bay of Biscay; and who, every now and again, stuns you with the thick end of the pole: the girl who does not skate with her hands in her muff; but who, throwing them up to heaven, says, "I'm going," and who goes, taking care that you go with her: the girl who, as you brush her down, and try to comfort her, explains to you indignantly that the horse took the corner too sharply and never noticed the mile-stone: the girl whose hair sea water does *not* improve.

There can be no doubt about it: that is where they keep the good woman of Fiction, where they keep the pretty girl of Art.

Does it not occur to you, *Messieurs les Auteurs*, that you are sadly disturbing us? These women that are a combination of Venus, St. Cecilia, and Elizabeth Fry! you paint them for us in your glowing pages: it is not kind of you, knowing, as you must, the women we have to put up with.

Would we not be happier, we men and women, were we to idealize one another less? My dear young lady, you have nothing whatever to complain to Fate about, I assure you. Unclasp those pretty hands of yours, and come away from the darkening window. Jack is as good a fellow as you deserve; don't yearn so much. Sir Galahad, my dear – Sir Galahad rides and fights in the land that lies beyond the sunset, far enough away from this noisy little earth where you and I spend much of our time tittle-tattling, flirting, wearing fine clothes, and going to shows. And besides, you must remember, Sir Galahad was a bachelor: as an idealist he was wise. Your Jack is by no means a bad sort of knight, as knights go nowadays in this un-idyllic world. There is much solid honesty about him, and he does not pose. He is not exceptional, I grant you; but, my dear, have you ever tried the exceptional man? Yes, he is very nice in a drawing-room, and it is interesting to read about him in the Society papers: you will find most of his good qualities *there*: take my advice, don't look into him too closely. You be content with Jack, and thank heaven he is no worse. We are not saints, we men – none of us, and our beautiful thoughts, I fear, we write in poetry not action. The White Knight, my dear young lady, with his pure soul, his heroic heart, his life's devotion to a noble endeavour, does not live down here to any great extent. They have tried it, one or two of them, and the world – you and I: the world is made up of you and I – has generally starved, and hooted them. There are not many of them left now: do you think you would care to be the wife of one, supposing one were to be found for you? Would you care to live with him in two furnished rooms in Clerkenwell, die with him on a chair bedstead? A century hence they will put up a statue of him, and you may be honoured as the wife who shared with him his sufferings. Do you think you are woman enough for that? If not, thank your stars you have secured, for your own exclusive use, one of us *un*exceptional men, who knows no better than to admire you. *You* are not exceptional.

And in us ordinary men there is some good. It wants finding, that is all. We are not so commonplace as you think us. Even your Jack, fond of his dinner, his conversation four-cornered by the Sporting Press – yes, I agree he is not interesting, as he sits snoring in the easy-chair; but, believe it or not, there are the makings of a great hero in Jack, if Fate would but be kinder to him, and shake him out of his ease.

Dr. Jekyll contained beneath his ample waistcoat not two egos, but three – not only Hyde but another, a greater than Jekyll – a man as near to the angels as Hyde was to the demons. These well-fed City men, these Gaiety Jonnies, these plough-boys, apothecaries, thieves! within each one lies hidden the hero, did Fate, the sculptor, choose to use his chisel. That little drab we have noticed now and then, our way taking us often past the end of the court, there was nothing by which to distinguish her. She was not over-clean, could use coarse language on occasion – just the spawn of the streets: take care lest the cloak of our child should brush her.

One morning the district Coroner, not, generally speaking, a poet himself, but an adept at discovering poetry buried under unlikely rubbish-heaps, tells us more about her. She earned six shillings a week, and upon it supported a bed-ridden mother and three younger children. She was housewife, nurse, mother, breadwinner, rolled into one. Yes, there are heroines *out* of fiction.

So loutish Tom has won the Victoric Cross – dashed out under a storm of bullets and rescued the riddled flag. Who would have thought it of loutish Tom? The village alehouse one always deemed the goal of his endeavours. Chance comes to Tom, and we find him out. To Harry the Fates were less kind. A ne'er-do-well was Harry – drank, knocked his wife about, they say. Bury him, we are well rid of him, he was good for nothing. Are we sure?

Let us acknowledge we are sinners. We know, those of us who dare to examine ourselves, that we are capable of every meanness, of every wrong under the sun. It is by the accident of circumstance, aided by the helpful watchfulness of the policeman, that our possibilities of crime are known only to ourselves. But having acknowledged our evil, let us also acknowledge that we are capable of greatness. The martyrs who faced death and torture unflinchingly for conscience' sake, were men and women like ourselves. They had their wrong side. Before the small trials of daily life they no doubt fell as we fall. By no means were they the pick of humanity. Thieves many of them had been, and murderers, evil-livers, and evil-doers. But the nobility was there also, lying dormant, and their day came. Among them must have been men who had cheated their neighbours over the counter; men who had been cruel to their wives and children; selfish, scandal-mongering women. In easier times their virtue might never have been known to any but their Maker.

In every age and in every period, when and where Fate has called upon men and women to play the man, human nature has not been found wanting. They were a poor lot, those French aristocrats that the Terror seized: cowardly, selfish, greedy had been their lives. Yet there must have been good, even in them. When the little things that in their little lives they had thought so great were swept away from them, when they found themselves face to face with the realities; then even they played the man. Poor shuffling Charles the First, crusted over with weakness and folly, deep down in him at last we find the great gentleman.

I like to hear stories of the littleness of great men. I like to think that Shakespeare was fond of his glass. I even cling to the tale of that disgraceful final orgie with friend Ben Jonson. Possibly the story may not be true, but I hope it was. I like to think of him as poacher, as village ne'er-do-well, denounced by the local grammar-school master, preached at by the local J.P. of the period. I like to reflect that Cromwell had a wart on his nose; the thought makes me more contented with my own features. I like to think that he put sweets upon the chairs, to see finely-dressed ladies spoil their frocks; to tell myself that he roared with laughter at the silly jest, like any East End 'Arry with his Bank Holiday squirt of dirty water. I like to read that Carlyle threw bacon at his wife, and occasionally made himself highly ridiculous over small annoyances, that would have been smiled at by a man of well-balanced mind. I think of the fifty foolish things a week *I* do, and say to myself, "I, too, am a literary man."

I like to think that even Judas had his moments of nobility, his good hours when he would willingly have laid down his life for his Master. Perhaps even to him there came, before the journey's end, the memory of a voice saying – "Thy sins be forgiven thee." There must have been good, even in Judas.

Virtue lies like the gold in quartz, there is not very much of it, and much pain has to be spent on the extracting of it. But Nature seems to think it worth her while to fashion these huge useless stones, if in them she may hide away her precious metals. Perhaps, also, in human nature, she cares little for the mass of dross, provided that by crushing and cleansing she can extract from it a little gold, sufficient to repay her for the labour of the world. We wonder why she troubles to make the stone. Why cannot the gold lie in nuggets on the surface? But her methods are secrets to us. Perchance there is a reason for the quartz. Perchance there is a reason for the evil and folly, through which run, unseen to the careless eye, the tiny veins of virtue.

Aye, the stone predominates, but the gold is there. We claim to have it valued. The evil that there is in man no tongue can tell. We are vile among the vile, a little evil people. But we are great. Pile up the bricks of our sins till the tower knocks at Heaven's gate, calling for vengeance, yet we are great – with a greatness and a virtue that the untempted angels may not reach to. The written history of the human race, it is one long record of cruelty, of falsehood, of oppression. Think you the world would be spinning round the sun unto this day, if that written record were all? Sodom, God would have spared had there been found ten righteous men within its walls. The world is saved by its just men. History sees them not; she is but the newspaper, a report of accidents. Judge you life by that? Then you shall believe that the true Temple of Hymen is the Divorce Court; that men are of two classes only, the thief and the policeman; that all noble thought is but a politician's catchword. History sees only the destroying conflagrations, she takes no thought of the sweet fire-sides. History notes the wrong; but the patient suffering, the heroic endeavour, that, slowly and silently, as the soft processes of Nature re-clothing with verdure the passion-wasted land, obliterate that wrong, she has no eyes for. In the days of cruelty and oppression – not altogether yet of the past, one fears – must have lived gentle-hearted men and women, healing with their help and sympathy the wounds that else the world had died of. After the thief, riding with jingle of sword and spur, comes, mounted on his ass, the good Samaritan. The pyramid of the world's evil – God help us! it rises high, shutting out almost the sun. But the record of man's good deeds, it lies written in the laughter of the children, in the light of lovers' eyes, in the dreams of the young men; it shall not be forgotten. The fires of persecution served as torches to show Heaven the heroism that was in man. From the soil of tyranny sprang self-sacrifice, and daring for the Right. Cruelty! what is it but the vile manure, making the ground ready for the flowers of tenderness and pity? Hate and Anger shriek to one another across the ages, but the voices of Love and Comfort are none the less existent that they speak in whispers, lips to ear.

We have done wrong, oh ye witnessing Heavens, but we have done good. We claim justice. We have laid down our lives for our friends: greater love hath no man than this. We have fought for the Right. We have died for the Truth – as the Truth seemed to us. We have done noble deeds; we have lived noble lives; we have comforted the sorrowful; we have succoured the weak. Failing, falling, making in our blindness many a false step, yet we have striven. For the sake of the army of just men and true, for the sake of the myriads of patient, loving women, for the sake of the pitiful and helpful, for the sake of the good that lies hidden within us, – spare us, O Lord.

ON THE MOTHERLINESS OF MAN

It was only a piece of broken glass. From its shape and colour, I should say it had, in its happier days, formed portion of a cheap scent-bottle. Lying isolated on the grass, shone upon by the early morning sun, it certainly appeared at its best. It attracted him.

He cocked his head, and looked at it with his right eye. Then he hopped round to the other side, and looked at it with his left eye. With either optic it seemed equally desirable.

That he was an inexperienced young rook goes without saying. An older bird would not have given a second glance to the thing. Indeed, one would have thought his own instinct might have told him that broken glass would be a mistake in a bird's nest. But its glitter drew him too strongly for resistance. I am inclined to suspect that at some time, during the growth of his family tree, there must have occurred a *mésalliance*, perhaps worse. Possibly a strain of magpie blood? – one knows the character of magpies, or rather their lack of character – and such things have happened. But I will not pursue further so painful a train: I throw out the suggestion as a possible explanation, that it all.

He hopped nearer. Was it a sweet illusion, this flashing fragment of rainbow; a beautiful vision to fade upon approach, typical of so much that is un-understandable in rook life? He made a dart forward and tapped it with his beak. No, it was real – as fine a lump of jagged green glass as any newly-married rook could desire, and to be had for the taking. *She* would be pleased with it. He was a well-meaning bird; the mere upward inclination of his tail suggested earnest though possibly ill-directed endeavour.

He turned it over. It was an awkward thing to carry; it had so very many corners. But he succeeded at last in getting it firmly between his beak, and in haste, lest some other bird should seek to dispute with him its possession, at once flew off with it.

A second rook who had been watching the proceedings from the lime tree, called to a third who was passing. Even with my limited knowledge of the language I found it easy to follow the conversation: it was so obvious.

"Issachar!"

"Hallo!"

"What do you think? Zebulan's found a piece of broken bottle. He's going to line his nest with it."

"No!"

"God's truth. Look at him. There he goes, he's got it in his beak."

"Well, I'm —!"

And they both burst into a laugh.

But Zebulan heeded them not. If he overheard, he probably put down the whole dialogue to jealousy. He made straight for his tree. By standing with my left cheek pressed close against the window-pane, I was able to follow him. He is building in what we call the Paddock elms – a suburb commenced only last season, but rapidly growing. I wanted to see what his wife would say.

At first she said nothing. He laid it carefully down on the branch near the half-finished nest, and she stretched up her head and looked at it.

Then she looked at him. For about a minute neither spoke. I could see that the situation was becoming strained. When she did open her beak, it was with a subdued tone, that had a vein of weariness running through it.

"What is it?" she asked.

He was evidently chilled by her manner. As I have explained, he is an inexperienced young rook. This is clearly his first wife, and he stands somewhat in awe of her.

"Well, I don't exactly know what it's *called*," he answered.

"Oh."

"No. But it's pretty, isn't it?" he added. He moved it, trying to get it where the sun might reach it. It was evident he was admitting to himself that, seen in the shade, it lost much of its charm.

"Oh, yes; very pretty," was the rejoinder; "perhaps you'll tell me what you're going to do with it."

The question further discomforted him. It was growing upon him that this thing was not going to be the success he had anticipated. It would be necessary to proceed warily.

"Of course, it's not a twig," he began.

"I see it isn't."

"No. You see, the nest is nearly all twigs as it is, and I thought —"

"Oh, you did think."

"Yes, my dear. I thought – unless you are of opinion that it's too showy – I thought we might work it in somewhere."

Then she flared out.

"Oh, did you? You thought that a good idea. An A1 prize idiot I seem to have married, I do. You've been gone twenty minutes, and you bring me back an eight- cornered piece of broken glass, which you think we might 'work into' the nest. You'd like to see me sitting on it for a month, you would. You think it would make a nice bed for the children to lie on. You don't think you could manage to find a packet of mixed pins if you went down again, I suppose? They'd look pretty 'worked in' somewhere, don't you think? – Here, get out of my way. I'll finish this nest by myself." She always had been short with him.

She caught up the offending object – it was a fairly

heavy lump of glass – and flung it out of the tree with all her force. I heard it crash through the cucumber frame. That makes the seventh pane of glass broken in that cucumber frame this week. The couple in the branch above are the worst. Their plan of building is the most extravagant, the most absurd I ever heard of. They hoist up ten times as much material as they can possibly use; you might think they were going to build a block, and let it out in flats to the other rooks. Then what they don't want they fling down again. Suppose we built on such a principle? Suppose a human husband and wife were to start erecting their house in Piccadilly Circus, let us say; and suppose the man spent all the day steadily carrying bricks up the ladder while his wife laid them, never asking her how many she wanted, whether she didn't think he had brought up sufficient, but just accumulating bricks in a senseless fashion, bringing up every brick he could find. And then suppose, when evening came, and looking round, they found they had some twenty cart-loads of bricks lying unused upon the scaffold, they were to commence flinging them down into Waterloo Place. They would get themselves into trouble; somebody would be sure to speak to them about it. Yet that is precisely what those birds do, and nobody says a word to them. They are supposed to have a President. He lives by himself in the yew tree outside the morning-room window. What I want know is what he is supposed to be good for. This is the sort of thing I want him to look into. I would like him to be worming underneath one evening when those two birds are tidying up: perhaps he would do something then. I have done all I can. I have thrown stones at them, that, in the course of nature, have returned to earth again, breaking more glass. I have blazed at them with a revolver; but they have come to regard this proceeding as a mere expression of light-heartedness on my part, possibly confusing me with the Arab of the Desert, who, I am given to understand, expresses himself thus in moments of deep emotion. They merely retire to a safe distance to watch me; no doubt regarding me as a poor performer, inasmuch as I do not also dance and shout between each shot. I have no objection to their building there, if they only would build sensibly. I want somebody to speak to them to whom they will pay attention.

You can hear them in the evening, discussing the matter of this surplus stock.

"Don't you work any more," he says, as he comes up with the last load, "you'll tire yourself."

"Well, I am feeling a bit done up," she answers, as she hops out of the nest and straightens her back.

"You're a bit peckish, too, I expect," he adds sympathetically. "I know I am. We will have a scratch down, and be off."

"What about all this stuff?" she asks, while titivating herself; "we'd better not leave it about, it looks so untidy."

"Oh, we'll soon get rid of that," he answers. "I'll have that down in a jiffy."

To help him, she seizes a stick and is about to drop it. He darts forward and snatches it from her.

"Don't you waste that one," he cries, "that's a rare one, that is. You see me hit the old man with it."

And he does. What the gardener says, I will leave you to imagine.

Judged from its structure, the rook family is supposed to come next in intelligence to man himself. Judging from the intelligence displayed by members of certain human families with whom I have come in contact, I can quite believe it. That rooks talk I am positive. No one can spend half-an-hour watching a rookery without being convinced of this. Whether the talk be always wise and witty, I am not prepared to maintain; but that there is a good deal of it is certain. A young French gentleman of my acquaintance, who visited England to study the language, told me that the impression made upon him by his first social evening in London was that of a parrot-house. Later on, when he came to comprehend, he, of course, recognized the brilliancy and depth of the average London drawing-room talk; but that is how, not comprehending, it impressed him at first. Listening to the riot of a rookery is much the same experience. The conversation to us sounds meaningless; the rooks themselves would probably describe it as sparkling.

There is a Misanthrope I know who hardly ever goes into Society. I argued the question with him one day. "Why should I?" he replied; "I know, say, a dozen men and women with whom intercourse is a pleasure; they have ideas of their own which they are not afraid to voice. To rub brains with such is a rare and goodly thing, and I thank Heaven for their friendship; but they are sufficient for my leisure. What more do I require? What is this 'Society' of which you all make so much ado? I have sampled it, and I find it unsatisfying. Analyze it into its elements, what is it? Some person I know very slightly, who knows me very slightly, asks me to what you call an 'At Home.' The evening comes, I have done my day's work and I have dined. I have been to a theatre or concert, or I have spent a pleasant hour or so with a friend. I am more inclined for bed than anything else, but I pull myself together, dress, and drive to the house. While I am taking off my hat and coat in the hall, a man enters I met a few hours ago at the Club. He is a man I have very little opinion of, and he, probably, takes a similar view of me. Our minds have no thought in common, but as it is necessary to talk, I tell him it is a warm evening. Perhaps it is a warm evening, perhaps it isn't; in either case he agrees with me. I ask him if he is going to Ascot. I do not care a straw whether he is going to Ascot or not. He says he is not quite sure, but asks me what chance Passion Flower has for the Thousand Guineas. I know he doesn't value my opinion on the subject at a brass farthing – he would be a fool if he did, but I cudgel my brains to reply to him, as though he were going to stake his shirt on my advice. We reach the first floor, and are mutually glad to get rid of one another. I catch my hostess' eye. She looks tired and worried; she would be happier in bed, only she doesn't know it. She smiles sweetly, but it is clear she has not the slightest idea who I am, and is waiting to catch my name from the butler. I whisper it to him. Perhaps he will get it right, perhaps he won't; it is quite immaterial. They have asked two hundred and forty guests, some seventy-five of whom they know by sight, for the rest, any chance passer-by, able, as the theatrical advertisements say, 'to dress and behave as a gentleman,' would do every bit as well. Indeed, I sometimes wonder why people go to the trouble and expense of invitation cards at all. A sandwich-man outside the door would answer the purpose. 'Lady Tompkins, At Home this afternoon from three to seven; Tea and Music. Ladies and Gentlemen admitted on presentation of visiting card. Afternoon dress indispensable.' The crowd is the thing wanted; as for the items, well, tell me, what is the difference, from the Society point of view, between one man in a black frock-coat and another?

"I remember being once invited to a party at a house in Lancaster Gate. I had met the woman at a picnic. In the same green frock and parasol I might have recognized her the next time I saw her. In any other clothes I did not expect to. My cabman took me to the house opposite, where they were also giving a party. It made no difference to any of us. The hostess – I never learnt her name – said it was very good of me to come, and then shunted me off on to a Colonial Premier (I did not catch his name, and he did not catch mine, which was not extraordinary, seeing that my hostess did not know it) who, she whispered to me, had come over from wherever it was (she did not seem to be very sure) principally to make my acquaintance. Half through the evening, and by accident, I discovered my mistake, but judged it too late to say anything then. I met a couple of people I knew, had a little supper with them, and came away. The next afternoon I met my right hostess – the lady who should have been my hostess. She thanked me effusively for having sacrificed the previous evening to her and her friends; she said she knew how seldom I went out: that made her feel my kindness all the more. She told me that the Brazilian Minister's wife had told her that I was the cleverest man she had ever met. I often think I should like to meet that man, whoever he may be, and thank him.

"But perhaps the butler does pronounce my name rightly, and perhaps my hostess actually does recognize me. She smiles, and says she was so afraid I was not coming. She implies that all the other guests are but as a feather in her scales of joy compared with myself. I smile in return, wondering to myself how I look when I do smile. I have never had the courage to face my own smile in the looking-glass. I notice the Society smile of other men, and it is not reassuring. I murmur something about my not having been likely to forget this evening; in my turn, seeking to imply that I have been looking forward to it for weeks. A few men shine at this sort of thing, but they are a small percentage, and without conceit I regard myself as no bigger a fool than the average male. Not knowing what else to say, I tell her also that it is a warm evening. She smiles archly as though there were some hidden witticism in the remark, and I drift away, feeling ashamed of myself. To talk as an idiot when you *are* an idiot brings no discomfort; to behave as an idiot when you have sufficient sense to know it, is painful. I hide myself in the crowd, and perhaps I'll meet a woman I was introduced to three weeks ago at a picture gallery. We don't know each other's names, but, both of us feeling lonesome, we converse, as it is called. If she be the ordinary type of woman, she asks me if I am going on to the Johnsons'. I tell her no. We stand silent for a moment, both thinking what next to say. She asks me if I was at the Thompsons' the day before yesterday. I again tell her no. I begin to feel dissatisfied with myself that I was not at the Thompsons'. Trying to get even with her, I ask her if she is going to the Browns' next Monday. (There are no Browns', she will have to say, No.) She is not, and her tone suggests that a social stigma rests upon the Browns. I ask her if she has been to Barnum's Circus; she hasn't, but is going. I give her my impressions of Barnum's Circus, which are precisely the impressions of everybody else who has seen the show.

"Or if luck be against me, she is possibly a smart woman, that is to say, her conversation is a running fire of spiteful remarks at the expense of every one she knows, and of sneers at the expense of every one she doesn't. I always feel I could make a better woman myself, out of a bottle of vinegar and a penn'orth of mixed pins. Yet it usually takes one about ten minutes to get away from her.

"Even when, by chance, one meets a flesh-and-blood man or woman at such gatherings, it is not the time or place for real conversation; and as for the shadows, what person in their senses would exhaust a single brain cell upon such? I remember a discussion once concerning Tennyson, considered as a social item. The dullest and most densely-stupid bore I ever came across was telling how he had sat next to Tennyson at dinner. 'I found him a most uninteresting man,' so he confided to us; 'he had nothing to say for himself – absolutely nothing.' I should like to resuscitate Dr. Samuel Johnson for an evening, and throw him into one of these 'At Homes' of yours."

My friend is an admitted misanthrope, as I have explained; but one cannot dismiss him as altogether unjust. That there is a certain mystery about Society's craving for Society must be admitted. I stood one evening trying to force my way into the supper room of a house in Berkeley Square. A lady, hot and weary, a few yards in front of me was struggling to the same goal.

"Why," remarked she to her companion, "why do we come to these places, and fight like a Bank Holiday crowd for eighteenpenny-worth of food?"

"We come here," replied the man, whom I judged to be a philosopher, "to say we've been here."

I met A—— the other evening, and asked him to dine with me on Monday. I don't know why I ask A—— to dine with me, but about once a month I do. He is an uninteresting man.

"I can't," he said, "I've got to go to the B——s'; confounded nuisance, it will be infernally dull."

"Why go?" I asked.

"I really don't know," he replied.

A little later B—— met me, and asked me to dine with him on Monday.

"I can't," I answered, "some friends are coming to us that evening. It's a duty dinner, you know the sort of thing."

"I wish you could have managed it," he said, "I shall have no one to talk to. The A—— s are coming, and they bore me to death."

"Why do you ask him?" I suggested.

"Upon my word, I really don't know," he replied.

But to return to our rooks. We were speaking of their social instincts. Some dozen of them – the "scallywags" and bachelors of the community, I judge them to be – have started a Club. For a month past I have been trying to understand what the affair was. Now I know: it is a Club.

And for their Club House they have chosen, of course, the tree nearest my bedroom window. I can guess how that came about; it was my own fault, I never thought of it. About two months ago, a single rook – suffering from indigestion or an unhappy marriage, I know not – chose this tree one night for purposes of reflection. He woke me up: I felt angry. I opened the window, and threw an empty soda-water bottle at him. Of course it did not hit him, and finding nothing else to throw, I shouted at him, thinking to frighten him away. He took no notice, but went on talking to himself. I shouted louder, and woke up my own dog. The dog barked furiously, and woke up most things within a quarter of a mile. I had to go down with a boot-jack – the only thing I could find handy – to soothe the dog. Two hours later I fell asleep from exhaustion. I left the rook still cawing.

The next night he came again. I should say he was a

bird with a sense of humour. Thinking this might happen, I had, however, taken the precaution to have a few stones ready. I opened the window wide, and fired them one after another into the tree. After I had closed the window, he hopped down nearer, and cawed louder than ever. I think he wanted me to throw more stones at him: he appeared to regard the whole proceeding as a game. On the third night, as I heard nothing of him, I flattered myself that, in spite of his bravado, I had discouraged him. I might have known rooks better.

What happened when the Club was being formed, I take it, was this:

"Where shall we fix upon for our Club House?" said the secretary, all other points having been disposed of. One suggested this tree, another suggested that. Then up spoke this particular rook:

"I'll tell you where," said he, "in the yew tree opposite the porch. And I'll tell you for why. Just about an hour before dawn a man comes to the window over the porch, dressed in the most comical costume you ever set eyes upon. I'll tell you what he reminds me of – those little statues that men use for decorating fields. He opens the window, and throws a lot of things out upon the lawn, and then he dances and sings. It's awfully interesting, and you can see it all from the yew tree."

That, I am convinced, is how the Club came to fix upon the tree next my window. I have had the satisfaction of denying them the exhibition they anticipated, and I cheer myself with the hope that they have visited their disappointment upon their misleader.

There is a difference between Rook Clubs and ours. In our clubs the respectable members arrive early, and leave at a reasonable hour; in Rook Clubs, it would appear, this principle is reversed. The Mad Hatter would have liked this Club – it would have been a club after his own heart. It opens at half-past two in the morning, and the first to arrive are the most disreputable members. In Rook-land the rowdy-dowdy, rand-dandy, rollicky-ranky boys get up very early in the morning and go to bed in the afternoon. Towards dawn, the older, more orderly members drop in for reasonable talk, and the Club becomes more respectable. The tree closes about six. For the first two hours, however, the goings-on are disgraceful. The proceedings, as often as not, open with a fight. If no two gentlemen can be found to oblige with a fight, the next noisiest thing to fall back upon is held to be a song. It is no satisfaction to me to be told that rooks cannot sing. *I* know that, without the trouble of referring to the natural history book. It is the rook who does not know it; *he* thinks he can; and as a matter of fact, he does. You can criticize his singing, you can call it what you like, but you can't stop it – at least, that is my experience. The song selected is sure to be one with a chorus. Towards the end it becomes mainly chorus, unless the soloist be an extra powerful bird, determined to insist upon his rights.

The President knows nothing of this Club. He gets up himself about seven – three hours after all the others have finished breakfast – and then fusses round under the impression that he is waking up the colony, the fat-headed old fool. He is the poorest thing in Presidents I have ever heard of. A South American Republic would supply a better article. The rooks themselves, the married majority, fathers of families, respectable nest-holders, are as indignant as I am. I hear complaints from all quarters.

Reflection comes to one as, towards the close of these chill afternoons in early spring, one leans upon the paddock gate watching the noisy bustling in the bare elms.

So the earth is growing green again, and love is come again unto the hearts of us old sober-coated fellows. Oh, Madam, your feathers gleam wondrous black, and your bonnie bright eye stabs deep. Come, sit by our side, and we'll tell you a tale such as rook never told before. It's the tale of a nest in a topmost bough, that sways in the good west wind. It's strong without, but it's soft within, where the little green eggs lie safe. And there sits in that nest a lady sweet, and she caws with joy, for, afar, she sees the rook she loves the best. Oh, he has been east, and he has been west, and his crop it is full of worms and slugs, and they are all for her.

We are old, old rooks, so many of us. The white is mingling with the purple black upon our breasts. We have seen these tall elms grow from saplings; we have seen the old trees fall and die. Yet each season come to us again the young thoughts. So we mate and build and gather that again our old, old hearts may quiver to the thin cry of our new-born.

Mother Nature has but one care, the children. We talk of Love as the Lord of Life: it is but the Minister. Our novels end where Nature's tale begins. The drama that our curtain falls upon, is but the prologue to her play. How the ancient Dame must laugh as she listens to the prattle of her children. "Is Marriage a Failure?" "Is Life worth Living?" "The New Woman *versus* the Old." So, perhaps, the waves of the Atlantic discuss vehemently whether they shall flow east or west.

Motherhood is the law of the Universe. The whole duty of man is to be a mother. We labour: to what end? the children – the woman in the home, the man in the community. The nation takes thought for its future: why? In a few years its statesmen, its soldiers, its merchants, its toilers, will be gathered unto their fathers. Why trouble we ourselves about the future? The country pours its blood and treasure into the earth that the children may reap. Foolish Jacques Bonhomie, his addled brain full of the maddest dreams, rushes with bloody hands to give his blood for Liberty. Equality, Fraternity. He will not live to see, except in vision, the new world he gives his bones to build – even his spinning word-whipped head knows that. But the children! they shall live sweeter lives. The peasant leaves his fireside to die upon the battle-field. What is it to him, a grain in the human sand, that Russia should conquer the East, that Germany should be united, that the English flag should wave above new lands? the heritage his fathers left him shall be greater for his sons. Patriotism! what is it but the mother instinct of a people?

Take it that the decree has gone forth from Heaven: There shall be no more generations, with this life the world shall die. Think you we should move another hand? The ships would rot in the harbours, the grain would rot in the ground. Should we paint pictures, write books, make music? hemmed in by that onward creeping sea of silence. Think you with what eyes husband and wife would look on one another. Think you of the wooing – the spring of Love dried up; love only a pool of stagnant water.

How little we seem to realize this foundation of our life. Herein, if nowhere else, lies our eternity. This Ego shall never die – unless the human race from beginning to end be but a passing jest of the Gods, to be swept aside when wearied of, leaving room for new experiments. These features of mine – we will not discuss their æsthetic value – shall never disappear; modified, varied, but in essential the same, they shall continue in ever increasing circles to the end of Time. This temperament of mine – this good and evil that is in me, it shall grow with every age, spreading ever wider, combining, amalgamating. I go into my children and my children's children: I am eternal. I am they, they are I. The tree withers and you clear the ground, thankful if out of its dead limbs you can make good firewood; but its spirit, its life, is in fifty saplings. The tree dies not, it changes.

These men and women that pass me in the street, this one hurrying to his office, this one to his club, another to his love, they are the mothers of the world to come.

This greedy trickster in stocks and shares, he cheats, he lies, he wrongs all men – for what? Follow him to his luxurious home in the suburbs: what do you find? A man with children on his knee, telling them stories, promising them toys. His anxious, sordid life, for what object is it lived? That these children may possess the things that he thinks good for them. Our very vices, side by side with our virtues, spring from this one root, Motherhood. It is the one seed of the Universe. The planets are but children of the sun, the moon but an offspring of the earth, stone of her stone, iron of her iron. What is the Great Centre of us all, life animate and inanimate – if any life *be* inanimate? Is the eternal universe one dim figure, Motherhood, filling all space?

This scheming Mother of Mayfair, angling for a rich son-in-law! Not a pleasing portrait to look upon, from one point of view. Let us look at it, for a moment, from another. How weary she must be! This is her third "function" to-night; the paint is running off her poor parched face. She has been snubbed a dozen times by her social superiors, openly insulted by a Duchess; yet she bears it with a patient smile. It is a pitiful ambition, hers: it is that her child shall marry money, shall have carriages and many servants, live in Park Lane, wear diamonds, see her name in the Society Papers. At whatever cost to herself, her daughter shall, if possible, enjoy these things. She could so much more comfortably go to bed, and leave the child to marry some well-to-do commercial traveller. Justice, Reader, even for such. Her sordid scheming is but the deformed child of Motherhood.

Motherhood! it is the gamut of God's orchestra, savageness and cruelty at the one end, tenderness and self-sacrifice at the other.

The sparrow-hawk fights the hen: he seeking food for his brood, she defending hers with her life. The spider sucks the fly to feed its myriad young; the cat tortures the mouse to give its still throbbing carcase to her kittens, and man wrongs man for children's sake. Perhaps when the riot of the world reaches us whole, not broken, we shall learn it is a harmony, each jangling discord fallen into its place around the central theme, Motherhood.

ON THE INADVISABILITY OF
FOLLOWING ADVICE

I was pacing the Euston platform late one winter's night, waiting for the last train to Watford, when I noticed a man cursing an automatic machine. Twice he shook his fist at it. I expected every moment to see him strike it. Naturally curious, I drew near softly. I wanted to catch what he was saying. However, he heard my approaching footsteps, and turned on me. "Are you the man," said he, "who was here just now?"

"Just where?" I replied. I had been pacing up and down the platform for about five minutes.

"Why here, where we are standing," he snapped out. "Where do you think 'here' is – over there?" He seemed irritable.

"I may have passed this spot in the course of my peregrinations, if that is what you mean," I replied. I spoke with studied politeness; my idea was to rebuke his rudeness.

"I mean," he answered, "are you the man that spoke to me, just a minute ago?"

"I am not that man," I said; "good-night."

"Are you sure?" he persisted.

"One is not likely to forget talking to you," I retorted. His tone had been most offensive. "I beg your pardon," he replied grudgingly. "I thought you looked like the man who spoke to me a minute or so ago."

I felt mollified; he was the only other man on the platform, and I had a quarter of an hour to wait. "No, it certainly wasn't me," I returned genially, but ungrammatically. "Why, did you want him?"

"Yes, I did," he answered. "I put a penny in the slot here," he continued, feeling apparently the need of unburdening himself; "I wanted a box of matches. I couldn't get anything out, and I was shaking the machine, and swearing at it, as one does, when there came along a man, about your size, and – you're *sure* it wasn't you?"

"Positive," I again ungrammatically replied; "I would tell you if it had been. What did he do?"

"Well, he saw what had happened, or guessed it. He said, 'They are troublesome things, those machines; they want understanding.' I said, 'They want taking up and flinging into the sea, that's what they want!' I was feeling mad because I hadn't a match about me, and I use a lot. He said, 'They stick sometimes; the thing to do is to put another penny in; the weight of the first penny is not always sufficient. The second penny loosens the drawer and tumbles out itself; so that you get your purchase together with your first penny back again. I have often succeeded that way.' Well, it seemed a silly explanation, but he talked as if he had been weaned by an automatic machine, and I was sawney enough to listen to him. I dropped in what I thought was another penny. I have just discovered it was a two-shilling piece. The fool was right to a certain extent; I have got something out. I have got this."

He held it towards me; I looked as it. It was a packet of Everton toffee.

"Two and a penny," he remarked, bitterly. "I'll sell it for a third of what it cost me."

"You have put your money into the wrong machine," I suggested.

"Well, I know that!" he answered, a little crossly, as it seemed to me – he was not a nice man: had there been any one else to talk to I should have left him. "It isn't losing the money I mind so much; it's getting this damn thing, that annoys me. If I could find that idiot I'd ram it down his throat."

We walked to the end of the platform, side by side, in silence.

"There are people like that," he broke out, as we turned, "people who will go about, giving advice. I'll be getting six months over one of them, I'm always afraid. I remember a pony I had once." (I judged the man to be a small farmer; he talked in a wurzelly tone. I don't know if you understand what I mean, but an atmosphere of wurzels was the thing that somehow he suggested.) "It was a thoroughbred Welsh pony, as sound a little beast as ever stepped. I'd had him out to grass all the winter, and one day in the early spring I thought I'd take him for a run. I had to go to Amersham on business. I put him into the cart, and drove him across; it is just ten miles from my place. He was a bit uppish, and had lathered himself pretty freely by the time we reached the town.

"A man was at the door of the hotel. He says, 'That's a good pony of yours.'

"'Pretty middling,' I says.

"'It doesn't do to over-drive 'em, when they're young,' he says.

"I says, 'He's done ten miles, and I've done most of the pulling. I reckon I'm a jolly sight more exhausted than he is.'

"I went inside and did my business, and when I came out the man was still there. 'Going back up the Hill?' he says to me.

"Somehow, I didn't cotton to him from the beginning. 'Well, I've got to get the other side of it,' I says, 'and unless you know any patent way of getting over a hill without going up it, I reckon I am.'

"He says, 'You take my advice: give him a pint of old ale before you start.'

"'Old ale,' I says; 'why he's a teetotaller.'

"'Never you mind that,' he answers; 'you give him a pint of old ale. I know these ponies; he's a good 'un, but he ain't set. A pint of old ale, and he'll take you up that hill like a cable tramway, and not hurt himself.'

"I don't know what it is about this class of man. One asks oneself afterwards why one didn't knock his hat over his eyes and run his head into the nearest horse-trough. But at the time one listens to them. I got a pint of old ale in a hand-bowl, and brought it out. About half-a-dozen chaps were standing round, and of course there was a good deal of chaff.

"'You're starting him on the downward course, Jim,' says one of them. 'He'll take to gambling, rob a bank, and burder his mother. That's always the result of a glass of ale, 'cording to the tracts.'

"'He won't drink it like that,' says another; 'it's as flat as ditch water. Put a head on it for him.'

"'Ain't you got a cigar for him?' says a third.

"'A cup of coffee and a round of buttered toast would do him a sight more good, a cold day like this,' says a fourth.

"I'd half a mind then to throw the stuff away, or drink it myself; it seemed a piece of bally nonsense, giving good ale to a four-year-old pony; but the moment the beggar smelt the bowl he reached out his head, and lapped it up as though he'd been a Christian; and I jumped into the cart and started off, amid cheers. We got up the hill pretty steady. Then the liquor began to work into his head. I've taken home a drunken man more than once, and there's pleasanter jobs than that. I've seen a drunken woman, and they're worse. But a drunken Welsh pony I never want to have anything more to do with so long as I live. Having four legs he managed to hold himself up; but as to guiding himself, he couldn't; and as for letting me do it, he wouldn't. First we were one side of the road, and then we were the other. When we were not either side, we were crossways in the middle. I heard a bicycle bell behind me, but I dared not turn my head. All I could do was to shout to the fellow to keep where he was.

"'I want to pass you,' he sang out, so soon as he was near enough.

"'Well, you can't do it,' I called back.

"'Why can't I?' he answered. 'How much of the road do *you* want?'

"'All of it, and a bit over,' I answered him, 'for this job, and nothing in the way.'

"He followed me for half-a-mile, abusing me; and every time he thought he saw a chance he tried to pass me. But the pony was always a bit too smart for him. You might have thought the brute was doing it on purpose.

"'You're not fit to be driving,' he shouted. He was quite right; I wasn't. I was feeling just about dead beat.

"'What do you think you are?' he continued, 'the charge of the Light Brigade?' (He was a common sort of fellow.) 'Who sent *you* home with the washing?'

"Well, he was making me wild by this time. 'What's the good of talking to me?' I shouted back. 'Come and blackguard the pony if you want to blackguard anybody. I've got all I can do without the help of that alarm clock of yours. Go away, you're only making him worse.'

"'What's the matter with the pony?' he called out.

"'Can't you see?' I answered. 'He's drunk.'

"Well, of course it sounded foolish; the truth often does.

"'One of you's drunk,' he retorted; 'for two pins I'd come and haul you out of the cart.'

"I wish to goodness he had; I'd have given something to be out of that cart. But he didn't have the chance. At that moment the pony gave a sudden swerve; and I take it he must have been a bit too close. I heard a yell and a curse, and at the same instant I was splashed from head to foot with ditch water. Then the brute bolted. A man was coming along, asleep on the top of a cart-load of windsor chairs. It's disgraceful the way those wagoners go to sleep; I wonder there are not more accidents. I don't think he ever knew what had happened to him. I couldn't look round to see what became of him; I only saw him start. Halfway down the hill a policeman holla'd to me to stop. I heard him shouting out something about furious driving. Half-a-mile this side of Chesham we came upon a girls' school walking two and two – a 'crocodile' they call it, I think. I bet you those girls are still talking about it. It must have taken the old woman a good hour to collect them together again.

"It was market-day in Chesham; and I guess there has not been a busier market-day in Chesham before or since. We went through the town at about thirty miles an hour. I've never seen Chesham so lively – it's a sleepy hole as a rule. A mile outside the town I sighted the High Wycombe coach. I didn't feel I minded much; I had got to that pass when it didn't seem to matter to me what happened; I only felt curious. A dozen yards off the coach the pony stopped dead; that jerked me off the seat to the bottom of the cart. I couldn't get up, because the seat was on top of me. I could see nothing but the sky, and occasionally the head of the pony, when he stood upon his hind legs. But I could hear what the driver of the coach said, and I judged he was having trouble also.

"'Take that damn circus out of the road,' he shouted. If he'd had any sense he'd have seen how helpless I was. I could hear his cattle plunging about; they are like that, horses – if they see one fool, then they all want to be fools.

"'Take it home, and tie it up to its organ,' shouted the guard.

"Then an old woman went into hysterics, and began laughing like an hyena. That started the pony off again, and, as far as I could calculate by watching the clouds, we did about another four miles at the gallop. Then he thought he'd try to jump a gate, and finding, I suppose, that the cart hampered him, he started kicking it to pieces. I'd never have thought a cart could have been separated into so many pieces, if I hadn't seen it done. When he had got rid of everything but half a wheel and the splashboard he bolted again. I remained behind with the other ruins, and glad I was to get a little rest. He came back later in the afternoon, and I was pleased to sell him the next week for a five-pound-note: it cost me about another ten to repair myself.

"To this day I am chaffed about that pony, and the local temperance society made a lecture out of me. That's what comes of following advice."

I sympathized with him. I have suffered from advice myself. I have a friend, a City man, whom I meet occasionally. One of his most ardent passions in life is to make my fortune. He button-holes me in Threadneedle Street. "The very man I wanted to see," he says; "I'm going to let you in for a good thing. We are getting up a little syndicate." He is for ever "getting up" a little syndicate, and for every hundred pounds you put into it you take a thousand out. Had I gone into all his little syndicates, I could have been worth at the present moment, I reckon, two million five hundred thousand pounds. But I have not gone into all his little syndicates. I went into one, years ago, when I was younger. I am still in it; my friend is confident that my holding, later on, will yield me thousands. Being, however, hard-up for ready money, I am willing to part with my share to any deserving person at a genuine reduction, upon a cash basis. Another friend of mine knows another man who is "in the know" as regards racing matters. I suppose most people posses a friend of this type. He is generally very popular just before a race, and extremely unpopular immediately afterwards. A third benefactor of mine is an enthusiast upon the subject of diet. One day he brought me something in a packet, and pressed it into my hand with the air of a man who is relieving you of all your troubles.

"What is it?" I asked.

"Open it and see," he answered, in the tone of a pantomime fairy.

I opened it and looked, but I was no wiser.

"It's tea," he explained.

"Oh!" I replied; "I was wondering if it could be snuff."

"Well, it's not exactly tea," he continued, "It's a sort of tea. You take one cup of that – one cup, and you will never care for any other kind of tea again."

He was quite right, I took one cup. After drinking it I felt I didn't care for any other tea. I felt I didn't care for anything, except to die quietly and inoffensively. He called on me a week later.

"You remember that tea I gave you?" he said.

"Distinctly," I answered; "I've got the taste of it in my mouth now."

"Did it upset you?" he asked.

"It annoyed me at the time," I answered; "but that's all over now."

He seemed thoughtful. "You were quite correct," he answered; "it *was* snuff, a very special snuff, sent me all the way from India."

"I can't say I liked it," I replied.

"A stupid mistake of mine," he went on – "I must have mixed up the packets."

"Oh, accidents will happen," I said, "and you won't make another mistake, I feel sure; so far as I am concerned."

We can all give advice. I had the honour once of serving an old gentleman whose profession it was to give legal advice, and excellent legal advice he always gave. In common with most men who know the law, he had little respect for it. I have heard him say to a would-be litigant –

"My dear sir, if a villain stopped me in the street and demanded of me my watch and chain, I should refuse to give it to him. If he thereupon said, 'Then I shall take it from you by brute force,' I should, old as I am, I feel convinced, reply to him, 'Come on.' But if, on the other hand, he were to say to me, 'Very well, then I shall take proceedings against you in the Court of Queen's Bench to compel you to give it up to me,' I should at once take it from my pocket, press it into his hand, and beg of him to say no more about the matter. And I should consider I was getting off cheaply."

Yet that same old gentleman went to law himself with his next-door neighbour over a dead poll parrot that wasn't worth sixpence to anybody, and spent from first to last a hundred pounds, if he spent a penny.

"I know I'm a fool," he confessed. "I have no positive proof that it *was* his cat; but I'll make him pay for calling me an Old Bailey Attorney, hanged if I don't!"

We all know how the pudding *ought* to be made. We do not profess to be able to make it: that is not our business. Our business is to criticize the cook. It seems our business to criticize so many things that it is not our business to do. We are all critics nowadays. I have my opinion of you, Reader, and you possibly have your own opinion of me. I do not seek to know it; personally, I prefer the man who says what he has to say of me behind my back. I remember, when on a lecturing tour, the ground-plan of the hall often necessitated my mingling with the audience as they streamed out. This never happened but I would overhear somebody in front of me whisper to his or her companion – "Take care, he's just behind you." I always felt so grateful to that whisper.

At a Bohemian Club, I was one drinking coffee with a Novelist, who happened to be a broad-shouldered, athletic man. A fellow-member, joining us, said to the Novelist, "I have just finished that last book of yours; I'll tell you my candid opinion of it." Promptly replied the Novelist, "I give you fair warning – if you do, I shall punch your head." We never heard that candid opinion.

Most of our leisure time we spend sneering at one another. It is a wonder, going about as we do with our noses so high in the air, we do not walk off this little round world into space, all of us. The Masses sneer at the Classes. The morals of the Classes are shocking. If only the Classes would consent as a body to be taught behaviour by a Committee of the Masses, how very much better it would be for them. If only the Classes would neglect their own interests and devote themselves to the welfare of the Masses, the Masses would be more pleased with them.

The Classes sneer at the Masses. If only the Masses would follow the advice given them by the Classes; if only they would be thrifty on their ten shillings a week; if only they would all be teetotallers, or drink old claret, which is not intoxicating; if only all the girls would be domestic servants on five pounds a year, and not waste their money on feathers; if only the men would be content to work for fourteen hours a day, and to sing in tune, "God bless the Squire and his relations," and would consent to be kept in their proper stations, all things would go swimmingly – for the Classes.

The New Woman pooh-poohs the Old; the Old woman is indignant with the New. The Chapel denounces the Stage; the Stage ridicules Little Bethel; the Minor Poet sneers at the world; the world laughs at the Minor Poet.

Man criticizes Woman. We are not altogether pleased with woman. We discuss her shortcomings, we advise her for her good. If only English wives would dress as French wives, talk as American wives, cook as German wives! if only women would be precisely what we want them to be – patient and hard-working, brilliantly witty and exhaustively domestic, bewitching, amenable, and less suspicious; how very much better it would be for them – also for us. We work so hard to teach them, but they will not listen. Instead of paying attention to our wise counsel, the tiresome creatures are wasting their time criticizing us. It is a popular game, this game of school. All that is needful is a doorstep, a cane, and six other children. The difficulty is the six other children. Every child wants to be the school-master; they will keep jumping up, saying it is their turn.

Woman wants to take the stick now, and put man on the doorstep. There are one or two things she has got to say to him. He is not at all the man she approves of. He must begin by getting rid of all his natural desires and propensities; that done, she will take him in hand and make of him – not a man, but something very much superior.

It would be the best of all possible worlds if everybody would only follow our advice. I wonder, would Jerusalem have been the cleanly city it is reported, if, instead of troubling himself concerning his own two-penny-halfpenny doorstep, each citizen had gone out into the road and given eloquent lectures to all the other inhabitants on the subject of sanitation?

We have taken to criticizing the Creator Himself of late. The world is wrong, we are wrong. If only he had taken our advice, during those first six days!

Why do I seem to have been scooped out and filled up with lead? Why do I hate the smell of bacon, and feel that nobody cares for me? It is because champagne and lobsters have been made wrong.

Why do Edwin and Angelina quarrel? It is because Edwin has been given a fine, high-spirited nature that will not brook contradiction; while Angelina, poor girl, has been cursed with contradictory instincts.

Why is excellent Mr. Jones brought down next door to beggary? Mr. Jones had an income of a thousand a year, secured by the Funds. But there came along a wicked Company promoter (why are wicked Company promoters permitted?) with a prospectus, telling good Mr. Jones how to obtain a hundred per cent. for his money by investing it in some scheme for the swindling of Mr. Jones's fellow-citizens.

The scheme does not succeed; the people swindled turn out, contrary to the promise of the prospectus, to be Mr. Jones and his fellow-investors. Why does Heaven allow these wrongs?

Why does Mrs. Brown leave her husband and children, to run off with the New Doctor? It is because an ill-advised Creator has given Mrs. Brown and the New Doctor unduly strong emotions. Neither Mrs.

Brown nor the New Doctor are to be blamed. If any human being be answerable it is, probably, Mrs. Brown's grandfather, or some early ancestor of the New Doctor's.

We shall criticize Heaven when we get there. I doubt if any of us will be pleased with the arrangements; we have grown so exceedingly critical.

It was once said of a very superior young man that he seemed to be under the impression that God Almighty had made the universe chiefly to hear what he would say about it. Consciously or unconsciously, most of us are of this way of thinking. It is an age of mutual improvement societies – a delightful idea, everybody's business being to improve everybody else; of amateur parliaments, of literary councils, of playgoers' clubs.

First Night criticism seems to have died out of late, the Student of the Drama having come to the conclusion, possibly, that plays are not worth criticizing. But in my young days we were very earnest at this work. We went to the play, less with the selfish desire of enjoying our evening, than with the noble aim of elevating the Stage. Maybe we did good, maybe we were needed – let us think so. Certain it is, many of the old absurdities have disappeared from the Theatre, and our rough-and-ready criticism may have helped the happy dispatch. A folly is often served by an unwise remedy.

The dramatist in those days had to reckon with his audience. Gallery and Pit took an interest in his work such as Galleries and Pits no longer take. I recollect witnessing the production of a very blood-curdling melodrama at, I think, the old Queen's Theatre. The heroine had been given by the author a quite unnecessary amount of conversation, so we considered. The woman, whenever she appeared on the stage, talked by the yard; she could not do a simple little thing like cursing the Villain under about twenty lines. When the hero asked her if she loved him, she stood up and made a speech about it that lasted three minutes by the watch. One dreaded to see her open her mouth. In the Third Act, somebody got hold of her and shut her up in a dungeon. He was not a nice man, speaking generally, but we felt he was the man for the situation, and the house cheered him to the echo. We flattered ourselves we had got rid of her for the rest of the evening. Then some fool of a turnkey came along, and she appealed to him, through the grating, to let her out for a few minutes. The turnkey, a good but soft-hearted man, hesitated.

"Don't you do it," shouted one earnest Student of the Drama, from the Gallery; "she's all right. Keep her there."

The old idiot paid no attention to our advice; he argued the matter to himself. "'Tis but a trifling request," he remarked; "and it will make her happy."

"Yes, but what about us?" replied the same voice from the Gallery. "You don't know her. You've only just come on; we've been listening to her all the evening. She's quiet now, you let her be."

"Oh, let me out, if only for one moment!" shrieked the poor woman. "I have something that I must say to my child."

"Write it on a bit of paper, and pass it out," suggested a voice from the Pit. "We'll see that he gets it."

"Shall I keep a mother from her dying child?" mused the turnkey. "No, it would be inhuman."

"No, it wouldn't" persisted the voice of the Pit; "not in this instance. It's too much talk that has made the poor child ill."

The turnkey would not be guided by us. He opened the cell door amidst the execrations of the whole house. She talked to her child for about five minutes, at the end of which time it died.

"Ah, he is dead!" shrieked the distressed parent.

"Lucky beggar!" was the unsympathetic rejoinder of the house.

Sometimes the criticism of the audience would take the form of remarks, addressed by one gentleman to another. We had been listening one night to a play in which action seemed to be unnecessarily subordinated to dialogue, and somewhat poor dialogue at that. Suddenly, across the wearying talk from the stage, came the stentorian whisper –

"Jim!"

"Hallo!"

"Wake me up when the play begins."

This was followed by an ostentatious sound as of snoring. Then the voice of the second speaker was heard –

"Sammy!"

His friend appeared to awake.

"Eh? Yes? What's up? Has anything happened?"

"Wake you up at half-past eleven in any event, I suppose?"

"Thanks, do, sonny." And the critic slept again.

Yes, we took an interest in our plays then. I wonder shall I ever enjoy the British Drama again as I enjoyed it in those days? Shall I ever enjoy a supper again as I enjoyed the tripe and onions washed down with bitter beer at the bar of the old Albion? I have tried many suppers after the theatre since then, and some, when friends have been in generous mood, have been expensive and elaborate. The cook may have come from Paris, his portrait may be in the illustrated papers; his salary may be reckoned by hundreds; but there is something wrong with his art, for all that, I miss a flavour in his meats. There is a sauce lacking.

Nature has her coinage, and demands payment in her own currency. At Nature's shop it is you yourself must pay. Your unearned increment, your inherited fortune, your luck, are not legal tenders across her counter.

You want a good appetite. Nature is quite willing to supply you. "Certainly, sir," she replies, "I can do you a very excellent article indeed. I have here a real genuine hunger and thirst that will make your meal a delight to you. You shall eat heartily and with zest, and you shall rise from the table refreshed, invigorated, and cheerful."

"Just the very thing I want," exclaims the gourmet delightedly. "Tell me the price."

"The price," answers Mrs. Nature, "is one long day's hard work."

The customer's face falls; he handles nervously his heavy purse.

"Cannot I pay for it in money?" he asks. "I don't like work, but I am a rich man, I can afford to keep French cooks, to purchase old wines."

Nature shakes her head.

"I cannot take your cheques, tissue and nerve are my charges. For these I can give you an appetite that will make a rump-steak and a tankard of ale more delicious to you than any dinner that the greatest *chef* in Europe could put before you. I can even promise you that a hunk of bread and cheese shall be a banquet to you; but you must pay my price in my money; I do not deal in yours."

And next the Dilettante enters, demanding a taste for Art and Literature, and this also Nature is quite prepared to supply.

"I can give you true delight in all these things," she answers. "Music shall be as wings to you, lifting you above the turmoil of the world. Through Art you shall catch a glimpse of Truth. Along the pleasant paths of Literature you shall walk as beside still waters."

"And your charge?" cries the delighted customer.

"These things are somewhat expensive," replies Nature. "I want from you a life lived simply, free from all desire of wordly success, a life from which passion has been lived out; a life to which appetite has been subdued."

"But you mistake, my dear lady," replies the Dilettante; "I have many friends, possessed of taste, and they are men who do not pay this price for it. Their houses are full of beautiful pictures, they rave about 'nocturnes' and 'symphonies,' their shelves are packed with first editions. Yet they are men of luxury and wealth and fashion. They trouble much concerning the making of money, and Society is their heaven. Cannot I be as one of these?"

"I do not deal in the tricks of apes," answers Nature

coldly; "the culture of these friends of yours is a mere pose, a fashion of the hour, their talk mere parrot chatter. Yes, you can purchase such culture as this, and pretty cheaply, but a passion for skittles would be of more service to you, and bring you more genuine enjoyment. My goods are of a different class. I fear we waste each other's time."

And next comes the boy, asking with a blush for love, and Nature's motherly old heart goes out to him, for it is an article she loves to sell, and she loves those who come to purchase it of her. So she leans across the counter, smiling, and tells him that she has the very thing he wants, and he, trembling with excitement, likewise asks the figure.

"It costs a good deal," explains Nature, but in no discouraging tone; "it is the most expensive thing in all my shop."

"I am rich," replies the lad. "My father worked hard and saved, and he has left me all his wealth. I have stocks and shares, and lands and factories; and will pay any price in reason for this thing."

But Nature, looking graver, lays her hand upon his arm.

"Put by your purse, boy," she says, "my price is not a price in reason, nor is gold the metal that I deal in. There are many shops in various streets where your bank-notes will be accepted. But if you will take an old woman's advice, you will not go to them. The thing they will sell you will bring sorrow and do evil to you. It is cheap enough, but, like all things cheap, it is not worth the buying. No man purchases it, only the fool."

"And what is the cost of the thing *you* sell then?" asks the lad.

"Self-forgetfulness, tenderness, strength," answers the old Dame; "the love of all things that are of good repute, the hate of all things evil – courage, sympathy, self-respect, these things purchase love. Put by your purse, lad, it will serve you in other ways, but it will not buy for you the goods upon my shelves."

"Then am I no better off than the poor man?" demands the lad.

"I know not wealth or poverty as you understand it," answers Nature. "Here I exchange realities only for realities. You ask for my treasures, I ask for your brain and heart in exchange – yours, boy, not your father's, not another's."

"And this price," he argues, "how shall I obtain it?"

"Go about the world," replies the great Lady. "Labour, suffer, help. Come back to me when you have earned your wages, and according to how much you bring me so we will do business."

Is real wealth so unevenly distributed as we think? Is not Fate the true Socialist? Who is the rich man, who the poor? Do we know? Does even the man himself know? Are we not striving for the shadow, missing the substance? Take life at its highest; which was the happier man, rich Solomon or poor Socrates? Solomon seems to have had most things that most men most desire – maybe too much of some for his own comfort. Socrates had little beyond what he carried about with him, but that was a good deal. According to our scales, Solomon should have been one of the happiest men that ever lived, Socrates one of the most wretched. But was it so?

Or taking life at its lowest, with pleasure its only goal. Is my lord Tom Noddy, in the stalls, so very much jollier than 'Arry in the gallery? Were beer ten shillings the bottle, and champagne fourpence a quart, which, think you, we should clamour for? If every West End Club had its skittle alley, and billiards could only be played in East End pubs, which game, my lord, would you select? Is the air of Berkeley Square so much more joy-giving than the atmosphere of Seven Dials? I find myself a piquancy in the air of Seven Dials, missing from Berkeley Square. Is there so vast a difference between horse-hair and straw, when you are tired? Is happiness multiplied by the number of rooms in one's house? Are Lady Ermintrude's lips so very much sweeter than Sally's of the Alley? What *is* success in life?

ON THE PLAYING OF MARCHES AT THE FUNERALS OF MARIONETTES

He began the day badly. He took me out and lost me. It would be so much better, would he consent to the usual arrangement, and allow me to take him out. I am far the abler leader: I say it without conceit. I am older than he is, and I am less excitable. I do not stop and talk with every person I meet, and then forget where I am. I do less to distract myself: I rarely fight, I never feel I want to run after cats, I take but little pleasure in frightening children. I have nothing to think about but the walk, and the getting home again. If, as I say, he would give up taking me out, and let me take him out, there would be less trouble all round. But into this I have never been able to persuade him.

He had mislaid me once or twice, but in Sloane Square he lost me entirely. When he loses me, he stands and barks for me. If only he would remain where he first barked, I might find my way to him; but, before I can cross the road, he is barking half-way down the next street. I am not so young as I was; and I sometimes think he exercises me more than is good for me. I could see him from where I was standing in the King's Road. Evidently he was most indignant. I was too far off to distinguish the barks, but I could guess what he was saying –

"Damn that man, he's off again."

He made inquiries of a passing dog –

"You haven't smelt my man about anywhere, have you?"

(A dog, of course, would never speak of *seeing* anybody or anything, smell being his leading sense. Reaching the top of a hill, he would say to his companion – "Lovely smell from here, I always think; I could sit and sniff here all the afternoon." Or, proposing a walk, he would say – "I like the road by the canal, don't you? There's something interesting to catch your nose at every turn.")

"No, I haven't smelt any man in particular," answered the other dog. "What sort of a smelling man is yours?"

"Oh, an egg-and-bacony sort of a man, with a dash of soap about him."

"That's nothing to go by," retorted the other; "most men would answer to that description, this time of the morning. Where were you when you last noticed him?"

At this moment he caught sight of me, and came up, pleased to find me, but vexed with me for having got lost.

"Oh, here you are," he barked; "didn't you see me go round the corner? Do keep closer. Bothered if half my time isn't taken up, finding you and losing you again."

The incident appeared to have made him bad-tempered; he was just in the humour for a row of any sort. At the top of Sloane Street, a stout military-looking gentleman started running after the Chelsea bus. With a "Hooroo" William Smith was after him. Had the old gentleman taken no notice, all would have been well. A butcher boy, driving just behind, would – I could read it in his eye – have caught Smith a flick as he darted into the road, which would have served him right; the old gentleman would have captured his bus; and the affair would have been ended. Unfortunately, he was that type of retired military man all gout and curry and no sense. He stopped to swear at the dog. That, of course, was what Smith wanted. It is not often he gets a scrimmage with a full-grown man. "They're a poor-spirited lot, most of them," he thinks; "they won't even answer you back. I like a man who shows a bit of pluck." He was frenzied with delight at his success. He flew round his victim, weaving whooping circles and curves that paralyzed the old gentleman as though they had been the mystic figures of a Merlin. The colonel clubbed his umbrella, and attempted to defend himself. I called to the dog, I gave good advice to the colonel (I judged him to be a colonel; the louder he spoke, the less one could understand him), but both were too excited to listen to me. A sympathetic bus driver leaned over, and whispered hoarse counsel.

"Ketch 'im by the tail, sir," he advised the old gentleman; "don't you be afraid of him; you ketch 'im firmly by the tail."

A milkman, on the other hand, sought rather to encourage Smith, shouting as he passed –

"Good dog, kill him!"

A child, brained within an inch by the old gentleman's umbrella, began to cry. The nurse told the old gentleman he was a fool – a remark which struck me as singularly apt. The old gentleman gasped back that perambulators were illegal on the pavement; and, between his exercises, inquired after myself. A crowd began to collect; and a policeman strolled up.

It was not the right thing: I do not defend myself; but, at this point, the temptation came to me to desert William Smith. He likes a street row, I don't. These things are matters of temperament. I have also noticed that he has the happy instinct of knowing when to disappear from a crisis, and the ability to do so; mysteriously turning up, quarter of a mile off, clad in a peaceful and pre-occupied air, and to all appearances another and a better dog.

Consoling myself with the reflection that I could be of no practical assistance to him; and remembering with some satisfaction that, by a fortunate accident, he was without his collar, which bears my name and address, I slipped round the off side of a Vauxhall bus, making no attempt at ostentation, and worked my way home through Lowndes Square and the Park.

Five minutes after I had sat down to lunch, he flung open the dining-room door, and marched in. It is his customary "entrance." In a previous state of existence, his soul was probably that of an Actor-Manager.

From his exuberant self-satisfaction, I was inclined to think he must have succeeded in following the milkman's advice; at all events, I have not seen the colonel since. His bad temper had disappeared, but his "uppishness" had, if possible, increased. Previous to his return, I had given The O'Shannon a biscuit. The O'Shannon had been insulted; he did not want a dog biscuit; if he could not have a grilled kidney he did not want anything. He had thrown the biscuit on the floor. Smith saw it and made for it. Now Smith never eats biscuits. I give him one occasionally, and he at once proceeds to hide it. He is a thrifty dog; he thinks of the future. "You never know what may happen," he says; "suppose the Guv'nor dies, or goes mad, or bankrupt, I may be glad even of this biscuit; I'll put it under the door-mat – no, I won't, somebody will find it there. I'll scratch a hole in the tennis lawn, and bury it there. That's a good idea; perhaps it'll grow." Once I caught him hiding it in my study, behind the shelf devoted to my own books. It offended me, his doing that; the argument was so palpable. Generally, wherever he hides it somebody finds it. We find it under our pillows – inside our boots; no place seems safe. This time he had said to himself – "By Jove! a whole row of the Guv'nor's books. Nobody will ever want to take these out; I'll hide it here." One feels a thing like that from one's own dog.

But The O'Shannon's biscuit was another matter. Honesty is the best policy; but dishonesty is the better fun. He made a dash for it, and commenced to devour it greedily; you might have thought he had not tasted food for a week.

The indignation of The O'Shannon was a sight for the gods. He has the good-nature of his race: had Smith asked him for the biscuit he would probably have given it to him; it was the insult – the immorality of the proceeding, that maddened The O'Shannon.

For a moment he was paralyzed.

"Well, of all the —— Did ye see that now?" he said to me with his eyes. Then he made a rush and snatched the biscuit out of Smith's very jaws. "Ye onprincipled black Saxon thief," growled The O'Shannon; "how dare ye take my biscuit?"

"You miserable Irish cur," growled Smith; "how was I to know it was your biscuit? Does everything on the floor belong to you? Perhaps you think I belong to you, I'm on the floor. I don't believe it is your biscuit, you long-eared, snubbed-nosed bog-trotter; give it me back."

"I don't require any of your argument, you flop-eared son of a tramp with half a tail," replied The O'Shannon. "You come and take it, if you think you are dog enough."

He did think he was dog enough. He is half the size of The O'Shannon, but such considerations weigh not with him. His argument is, if a dog is too big for you to fight the whole of him, take a bit of him and fight that. He generally gets licked, but what is left of him invariably swaggers about afterwards under the impression it is the victor. When he is dead, he will say to himself, as he settles himself in his grave – "Well, I flatter myself I've laid out that old world at last. It won't trouble *me* any more, I'm thinking."

On this occasion, *I* took a hand in the fight. It becomes necessary at intervals to remind Master Smith that the man, as the useful and faithful friend of dog, has his rights. I deemed such interval had arrived. He flung himself on to the sofa, muttering. It sounded like – "Wish I'd never got up this morning. Nobody understands me."

Nothing, however, sobers him for long. Half-an-hour later, he was killing the nextdoor cat. He will never learn sense; he has been killing that cat for the last three months. Why the next morning his nose his invariably twice its natural size, while for the next week he can see objects on one side of his head only, he never seems to grasp; I suppose he attributes it to change in the weather.

He ended up the afternoon with what he no doubt regarded as a complete and satisfying success. Dorothea had invited a lady to take tea with her that day. I heard the sound of laughter, and, being near the nursery, I looked in to see what was the joke. Smith was worrying a doll. I have rarely seen a more worried-looking doll. Its head was off, and its sawdust strewed the floor. Both the children were crowing with delight; Dorothea, in particular, was in an ecstacy of amusement.

"Whose doll is it?" I asked.

"Eva's," answered Dorothea, between her peals of laughter.

"Oh no, it isn't," explained Eva, in a tone of sweet content; "here's my doll." She had been sitting on it, and now drew it forth, warm but whole. "That's Dorry's doll."

The change from joy to grief on the part of Dorothea was distinctly dramatic. Even Smith, accustomed to storm, was nonplussed at the suddenness of the attack upon him.

Dorothea's sorrow lasted longer than I had expected. I promised her another doll. But it seemed she did not want another; that was the only doll she would ever care for so long as life lasted; no other doll could ever take its place; no other doll would be to her what that doll had been. These little people are so absurd: as if it could matter whether you loved one doll or another, when all are so much alike! They have curly hair, and pink-and-white complexions, big eyes that open and shut, a little red mouth, two little hands. Yet these foolish little people! they will love one, while another they will not look upon. I find the best plan is not to reason with them, but to sympathize. Later on – but not too soon – introduce to them another doll. They will not care for it at first, but in time they will come to take an interest in it. Of course, it cannot make them forget the first doll; no doll ever born in Lowther Arcadia could be as that, but still – It is many weeks before they forget entirely the first love.

We buried Dolly in the country under the yew tree. A friend of mine who plays the fiddle came down on purpose to assist. We buried her in the hot spring sunshine, while the birds from shady nooks sang joyously of life and love. And our chief mourner cried real tears, just for all the world as though it were not the fate of dolls, sooner or later, to get broken – the little fragile things, made for an hour, to be dressed and kissed; then, paintless and stript, to be thrown aside on the nursery floor. Poor little dolls! I wonder do they take themselves seriously, not knowing the springs that stir their sawdust bosoms are but clockwork, not seeing the wires to which they dance? Poor little marionettes! do they talk together, I wonder, when the lights of the booth are out?

You, little sister doll, were the heroine. You lived in the white-washed cottage, all honeysuckle and clematis without – earwiggy and damp within, maybe. How pretty you always looked in your simple, neatly-fitting print dress. How good you were! How nobly you bore your poverty. How patient you were under your many wrongs. You never harboured an evil thought, a revengeful wish – never, little doll? Were there never moments when you longed to play the wicked woman's part, live in a room with many doors, be-clad in furs and jewels, with lovers galore at your feet? In those long winter evenings? the household work is done – the greasy dishes washed, the floor scrubbed; the excellent child is asleep in the corner; the one-and-eleven-penny lamp sheds its dismal light on the darned table-cloth; you sit, busy at your coarse sewing, waiting for Hero Dick, knowing – guessing, at least, where he is —! Yes, dear, I remember your fine speeches, when you told her, in stirring language the gallery cheered to the echo, what you thought of her and of such women as she; when, lifting your hand to heaven, you declared you were happier in your attic, working your fingers to the bone, than she in her gilded salon – I think "gilded salon" was the term, was it not? – furnished by sin. But speaking of yourself, weak little sister doll, not of your fine speeches, the gallery listening, did you not, in your secret heart, envy her? Did you never, before blowing out the one candle, stand for a minute in front of the cracked glass, and think to yourself that you, too, would look well in low-cut dresses from Paris, the diamonds flashing on your white smooth skin? Did you never, toiling home through the mud, bearing your bundle of needlework, feel bitter with the wages of virtue, as she splashed you, passing by in her carriage? Alone, over your cup of weak tea, did you never feel tempted to pay the price for champagne suppers, and gaiety, and admiration? Ah, yes, it is easy for folks who have had their good time, to prepare copybooks for weary little inkstained fingers, longing for play. The fine maxims sound such cant when we are in that mood, do they not? You, too, were young and handsome: did the author of the play think you were never hungry for the good things of life? Did he think that reading tracts to crotchety old women was joy to a full-blooded girl in her twenties? Why should *she* have all the love, and all the laughter? How fortunate that the villain, the Wicked Baronet, never opened the cottage door at that moment, eh, dear! He always came when you were strong, when you felt that you could denounce him, and scorn his temptations. Would that the villain came to all of us at such time; then we would all, perhaps, be heroes and heroines.

Ah well, it was only a play: it is over now. You and I, little tired dolls, lying here side by side, waiting to know our next part, we can look back and laugh. Where is she, this wicked dolly, that made such a stir on our tiny stage? Ah, here you are, Madam; I thought you could not be far; they have thrown us all into this corner together. But how changed you are, Dolly: your paint rubbed off, your golden hair worn to a wisp. No wonder; it was a trying part you had to play. How tired you must have grown of the glare and the glitter! And even hope was denied you. The peace you so longed for you knew you had lost the power to enjoy. Like the girl bewitched in the fairy tale, you knew you must dance ever faster and faster, with limbs growing palsied, with face growing ashen, and hair growing grey, till Death should come to release you; and your only prayer was he might come ere your dancing grew comic.

Like the smell of the roses to Nancy, hawking them through the hot streets, must the stifling atmosphere of love have been to you. The song of passion, how monotonous in your ears, sung now by the young and now by the old; now shouted, now whined, now shrieked; but ever the one strident tune. Do you remember when first you heard it? You dreamt it the morning hymn of Heaven. You came to think it the dance music of Hell, ground from a cracked hurdy-gurdy, lent out by the Devil on hire.

An evil race we must have seemed to you, Dolly Faustine, as to some Old Bailey lawyer. You saw but one side of us. You lived in a world upside down, where the leaves and the blossoms were hidden, and only the roots saw your day. You imagined the worm-beslimed fibres the plant, and all things beautiful you deemed cant. Chivalry, love, honour! how you laughed at the lying words. You knew the truth – as you thought: aye, half the truth. We were swine while your spell was upon us, Daughter of Circe, and you, not knowing your island secret, deemed it our natural shape.

No wonder, Dolly, your battered waxen face is stamped with an angry sneer. The Hero, who eventually came into his estates amid the plaudits of the Pit, while you were left to die in the streets! you remembered, but the house had forgotten those earlier scenes in always wicked Paris. The good friend of the family, the breezy man of the world, the *Deus ex Machina* of the play, who was so good to everybody, whom everybody loved! aye,

you loved him once – but that was in the Prologue. In the
Play proper, he was respectable. (How you loathed that
word, that meant to you all you vainly longed for!) To
him the Prologue was a period past and dead; a memory,
giving flavour to his life. To you, it was the First Act of
the Play, shaping all the others. His sins the house had
forgotten: at yours, they held up their hands in horror.
No wonder the sneer lies on your waxen lips.

Never mind, Dolly; it was a stupid house. Next time,
perhaps, you will play a better part; and then they will
cheer, instead of hissing you. You were wasted, I am
inclined to think, on modern comedy. You should have
been cast for the heroine of some old-world tragedy. The
strength of character, the courage, the power of
self-forgetfulness, the enthusiasm were yours: it was the
part that was lacking. You might have worn the mantle of
a Judith, a Boadicea, or a Jeanne d'Arc, had such plays
been popular in your time. Perhaps they, had they played
in your day, might have had to be content with such a
part as yours. They could not have played the meek
heroine, and what else would there have been for them in
modern drama? Catherine of Russia! had she been a
waiter's daughter in the days of the Second Empire,
should we have called her Great? The Magdalene! had
her lodging in those days been in some bye-street of
Rome instead of in Jerusalem, should we mention her
name in our churches?

You were necessary, you see, Dolly, to the piece. We
cannot all play heroes and heroines. There must be
wicked people in the play, or it would not interest. Think
of it, Dolly, a play where all the women were virtuous, all
the men honest! We might close the booth; the world
would be as dull as an oyster-bed. Without you wicked
folk there would be no good. How should we have known
and honoured the heroine's worth, but by contrast with
your worthlessness? Where would have been her fine
speeches, but for you to listen to them? Where lay the
hero's strength, but in resisting temptation of you? Had

not you and the Wicked Baronet between you robbed him of his estates, falsely accused him of crime, he would have lived to the end of the play an idle, unheroic, incomplete existence. You brought him down to poverty; you made him earn his own bread – a most excellent thing for him; gave him the opportunity to play the man. But for your conduct in the Prologue, of what value would have been that fine scene at the end of the Third Act, that stirred the house to tears and laughter? You and your accomplice, the Wicked Baronet, made the play possible. How would Pit and Gallery have known they were virtuous, but for the indignation that came to them, watching your misdeeds? Pity, sympathy, excitement, all that goes to the making of a play, you were necessary for. It was ungrateful of the house to hiss you.

And you, Mr. Merryman, the painted grin worn from your pale lips, you too were dissatisfied, if I remember rightly, with your part. You wanted to make the people cry, not laugh. Was it a higher ambition? The poor tired people! so much happens in their life to make them weep, is it not good sport to make them merry for awhile? Do you remember that old soul in the front row of the Pit? How she laughed when you sat down on the pie! I thought she would have to be carried out. I heard her talking to her companion as they passed the stage-door on their way home. "I have not laughed, my dear, till to-night," she was saying, the good, gay tears still in her eyes, "since the day poor Sally died." Was not that alone worth the old stale tricks you so hated? Aye, they were commonplace and conventional, those antics of yours that made us laugh; are not the antics that make us weep commonplace and conventional also? Are not all the plays, played since the booth was opened, but of one pattern, the plot old-fashioned now, the scenes now commonplace? Hero, villain, cynic – are their parts so much the fresher. The love duets, are they so very new? The death-bed scenes, would you call them uncommonplace? Hate, and Evil, and Wrong – are *their* voices new to the booth? What are you waiting for, people? a play with a plot that is novel, with characters that have never strutted before? It will be ready for you, perhaps, when you are ready for it, with new tears and new laughter.

You, Mr. Merryman, were the true philosopher. You saved us from forgetting the reality when the fiction grew somewhat strenuous. How we all applauded your gag in answer to the hero, when, bewailing his sad fate, he demanded of Heaven how much longer he was to suffer evil fortune. "Well, there cannot be much more of it in store for you," you answered him, "it's nearly nine o'clock already, and the show closes at ten." And true to your prophecy the curtain fell at the time appointed, and his troubles were of the past. You showed us the truth behind the mask. When pompous Lord Shallow, in ermine and wig, went to take his seat amid the fawning crowd, you pulled the chair from under him, and down he sat plump on the floor. His robe flew open, his wig flew off. No longer he awed us. His aped dignity fell from him; we saw him a stupid-eyed, bald little man; he imposed no longer upon us. It is your fool who is the only true wise man.

Yours was the best part in the play, Brother Merryman, had you and the audience but known it. But you dreamt of a showier part, where you loved and fought. I have heard you now and again, when you did not know I was near, shouting with sword in hand before your looking-glass. You had thrown your motley aside to don a dingy red coat; you were the hero of the play, you performed the gallant deeds, you made the noble speeches. I wonder what the play would be like, were we all to write our own parts. There would be no clowns, no singing chambermaids. We would all be playing lead in the centre of the stage, with the lime-light exclusively devoted to ourselves. Would it not be so?

What grand acting parts they are, these characters we write for ourselves alone in our dressing-rooms. We are always brave and noble – wicked sometimes, but if so, in a great, high-minded way; never in a mean or little way. What wondrous deeds we do, while the house looks on and marvels. Now we are soldiers, leading armies to victory. What if we die: it is in the hour of triumph, and a nation is left to mourn. Not in some forgotten skirmish do we ever fall; not for some "affair of outposts" do we give our blood, our very name unmentioned in the dispatches home. Now we are passionate lovers, well losing a world for love – a very different thing to being a laughter-provoking co-respondent in a sordid divorce case.

And the house is always crowded when we play. Our fine speeches always fall on sympathetic ears, our brave deeds are noted and applauded. It is so different in the real performance. So often we play our parts to empty benches, or if a thin house be present, they misunderstand, and laugh at the pathetic passages. And when our finest opportunity comes, the royal box, in which *he* or *she* should be present to watch us, is vacant.

Poor little dolls, how seriously we take ourselves, not knowing the springs that stir our bosoms are but clockwork, not seeing the wires to which we dance. Poor little marionettes, shall we talk together, I wonder, when the lights of the booth are out?

We are little wax dollies with hearts. We are little tin soldiers with souls. Oh, King of many toys, are you merely playing with us? *Is* it only clockwork within us, this thing that throbs and aches? Have you wound us up but to let us run down? Will you wind us again to-morrow, or leave us here to rust? *Is* it only clockwork to which we respond and quiver? Now we laugh, now we cry, now we dance; our little arms go out to clasp one another, our little lips kiss, then say good-bye. We strive, and we strain, and we struggle. We reach now for gold, now for laurel. We call it desire and ambition: are they only wires that you play? Will you throw the clockwork aside, or use it again, O Master?

The lights of the booth grow dim. The springs are broken that kept our eyes awake. The wire that held us erect is snapped, and helpless we fall in a heap on the stage. Oh, brother and sister dollies we played beside, where are you? Why is it so dark and silent? Why are we being put into this black box? And hark! the little doll orchestra — how far away the music sounds! what is it they are playing:—

THE END